FPL
Y
796.352
B+T

FRAMINGHAM PUBLIC LIBRARY

JAN 1 8 2001

FRAMINGHAM PUBLIC LIBRARY

"A-GAME"
GOLF

**Also by John Andrisani**

*The Tiger Woods Way*

*The Short Game Magic of Tiger Woods*

*The Ben Hogan Way*

# LF

**THE COMPLETE STARTER KIT FOR GOLFERS FROM TIGER WOODS' AMATEUR INSTRUCTOR**

JOHN ANSELMO WITH JOHN ANDRISANI

FOREWORD BY EARL WOODS

DOUBLEDAY

NEW YORK  LONDON  TORONTO  SYDNEY  AUCKLAND

PUBLISHED BY DOUBLEDAY

a division of Random House, Inc.

1540 Broadway, New York, New York 10036

DOUBLEDAY and the portrayal of an anchor with a dolphin are

trademarks of Doubleday, a division of Random House, Inc.

Library of Congress Cataloging-in-Publication Data

Anselmo, John.

A-game golf: the complete starter kit for golfers from Tiger Woods' amateur instructor /

John Andrisani; foreword by Earl Woods.—1st ed.

p.      cm

1. Golf for children—Study and teaching.    2. Woods, Tiger.

I. Andrisani, John.    II. Title.

GV966.3 .A58 2001

796.352—dc21

00-048608

ISBN 0-385-49813-6

Copyright © 2001 by John Anselmo

All Rights Reserved

Printed in the United States of America

June 2001

FIRST EDITION

*Designed by Lee Fukui*

1 3 5 7 9 10 8 6 4 2

*I dedicate this book to my greatest*

*student ever—Tiger Woods—and to*

*all the other players who practice*

*hard and intelligently and continue*

*to set a good example for a nation of*

*golfers searching to improve their*

*scores and enjoy the game more.*

# CONTENTS

# FOREWORD

All of the golf championships won by my son, Eldrick "Tiger" Woods, both as an amateur and as a pro, at home and at tournament venues afar, have brought great joy to me and my wife, Tida. Our family home in Cypress, California, is filled with trophies that remind us of Tiger's talents. He was a great junior player—the best ever. Of course, too, his three U.S. Amateur trophies mark a highlight in his career. And I'll never forget how happy our family was when we watched Tiger win his first two major championships, the Masters in 1997 and the PGA in 1999. Having said that, his last two major championship victories, in the New Millennium, were something very special.

I was thrilled to watch Tiger win the 2000 United States Open, the most prestigious golf championship held on our shores and undoubtedly the most difficult to win. It always draws a field of great players from around the world. Plus, the course is always set up to test a player—long holes, narrow fairways, deep rough, heavy fringe grass, and fast, tricky greens. When Tiger held the U.S. Open trophy high above his head, I felt the urge to salute my son, whose victory triggered a tremendous feeling of patriotism in my heart. And, oh boy, when Tiger won the next great major championship, the 2000 British Open, I jumped for joy.

In reigning victorious in "the British," Tiger became the youngest player to win the Grand Slam and joined the company of the few other golfing legends who have also won "The Slam"—Gene Sarazen, Ben Hogan, Jack Nicklaus, and Gary Player.

Many sportswriters are quick to call Tiger a "phenom," and they are not wrong in their assessment. There is no doubt that Tiger was born with good genes. However, let me also confirm that Tiger practiced very hard to become the superstar golfer he is today.

When Tiger was an infant he sat in a high chair and watched me hit shots into a net set up in the garage of our home. Every once in a while I would glance back out of the corner of my eye to check on Tiger, only to find him staring at the club in my hands, his eyes big as marbles, waiting for me to make the next swing. It was clearly evident that Tiger was very curious about the mechanics of the swing and the ins and outs of what made my technique tick. Oh, boy, did he get excited when the club hit the ball powerfully into the net. Even back then I could see that he was anxious to jump down from his perch and give golf a go.

Little did I know that there would be such a short gap between the time Tiger first watched me hit balls and when he actually swung the club himself. To shorten a long story, when Tiger was ten months old he climbed down from his high chair and hit the ball into the net. All I could do was yell to my wife, "Honey, get in here quick, look at this!" My wife and I were truly amazed—rather shocked—that Tiger had learned so much so fast about the golf swing. Consequently, soon after we gave him a cut-down putter so he could hit balls into the net (just like Dad). I also began teaching him the basics of the setup, namely the important elements of grip, stance, aim, and alignment. I let Tiger swing by feel, figuring that giving him that freedom was far better than flooding his head with various technical keys that would inevitably block him from feeding off any innate talents.

As was well documented in my book, *Training A Tiger,* I could see early on that my son was indeed gifted. The world got to see just how special Tiger's swing was when he made his first television appearance, at age three, on *The Mike Douglas Show,* and at age five on *That's Incredible.* But, Tiger didn't have just a good swing, he could hit the ball at a target consistently, as evidenced by the hole-in-one he scored at age eight. At that same age he won his first Junior World Championship, further indicating that he knew how to hit fairways and greens and get the ball in the hole from around the green and on it.

I am proud of the way I handled Tiger during his very early years. But I am even more proud of what Tiger has accomplished since. Again, I am especially proud of Tiger's U.S. Open and British Open wins, in the year 2000, for a few reasons.

Over the four days at Pebble Beach, venue for the 2000 U.S. Open, Tiger showed a sense of maturity both as a person and as a player. When he hit a bad shot or got a bad break—and admittedly there were few—he almost always kept his cool and carried on like a man. The shots he hit were fantastic, particularly his power shots off the tee, his precise irons into the greens, his super recovery shots from the rough, and his birdie- and par-saving putts. After winning by fifteen strokes there was no doubt in my mind or anybody else's that Tiger had brought his A-game swing and mind-set to "Pebble" and gotten the job done. He had it all!

Over the four days at St. Andrews, site for the 2000 British Open, Tiger acted like a true man on the course, staying extremely focused and calm throughout the event. Winning by eight shots, he proved he was the best golfer in the world.

It would be unfair of me to take all of the credit for molding Tiger into a champion, since other key players have been involved in the evolution of Tiger and his rise to stardom. My wife played a major role in helping Tiger develop a positive attitude, while sports psychologist Jay Brunza played a large part in teaching Tiger how to concentrate intently, imagine a perfectly played shot, and deal with the occasional bad bounce or bad day. Golf pro Rudy Duran deserves credit for taking over the reins from me and giving Tiger tips on improving his swing from the time he was five years old until he was ten. At that point teaching genius John Anselmo took over. I asked John to train my son, and he did a miraculous job. When Tiger turned eighteen he began taking lessons from Butch Harmon, another master instructor, who still coaches him. I believe that John's expertise and insights on the game greatly benefited Tiger in those formative years. If you don't believe me, here's what Tiger said when interviewed on The Golf Channel.

*"It's unbelievable how John kept things fun and interesting, while changing my swing plane, from flat to upright, and teaching me a new shot practically every time he gave me a lesson on the tee or on the course."*

Because of the extremely positive influence my dear friend John has had on Tiger, and the great knowledge he has shared with him, I was pleased to hear that he wrote *"A-Game" Golf.* I can't guarantee that by reading this book you will achieve a scratch handicap, or that his tips will turn your son or daughter into a world champion golfer. All the same I do guarantee that any golfer who pays attention to John's instructional messages, swing philosophy, and shot-making secrets is bound to improve and enjoy the game more. The reason, in a nutshell: John's method for swinging the club and hitting shots is simple and easy to repeat because it caters to our natural instincts.

—Earl Woods

# ACKNOWLEDGMENTS

I thank my agent Scott Waxman for ushering *"A-Game" Golf* into the very capable hands of Shawn Coyne, senior editor at Doubleday, who believed in the project and helped make the book as good as it could possibly be.

Someone else who had a great deal to do with the direction of this book was John Andrisani, a former golf teacher and expert instructional writer best known for his work with top players and coaches. John had already written two books analyzing Tiger Woods' power-swing and short game, so I knew that he was the ideal person to coauthor what I consider my instructional magnum opus.

As fine a player as Tiger is, this book is not only about my experiences with him on the lesson tee and golf course. I learned a lot from teaching Tiger, but also from instructing Kim Saiki, a multiple winner on the amateur circuit who is now an LPGA player, Kelly Manos, Bobby Clark, Ruth Miller, Candy Myers, and Harriet Glanville. I continue to learn a lot from amateur and pro students, most notably Robert Kramer, who is now eighteen years old, and juniors Billy Olsen and Dennis Chang. All these students plus Dan and Alexandra Anselmo and Billy Olsen's father were kind enough to be photographic models for *"A-Game" Golf.*

John Anselmo cherishes the "Team Tiger" shirt given to him by Kultida (Tida) Woods, Tiger's mother.

I am grateful to Tiger and all my students for helping me confirm what works best in the golf swing. Just about everything I have learned about golf technique, from my students, fellow teaching pros, and legends such as Sam Snead and Ben Hogan, will be shared with you in *"A-Game" Golf.* I'll even share with you the equipment secrets I learned from Bill Orr, who constantly worked on Tiger's clubs when he really grew between the ages of thirteen and fifteen. So, no matter what your age, you can use this book as a guiding light to improvement.

Since photographs and artwork are very important to clearly relaying the instructional message, I owe thanks to those who contributed. I am grateful to the book's main photographer, Yasuhiro Tanabe and, too, artist Allen Welkis. Additionally, I owe thanks to the Woods family, who were kind enough to let me use some "takes" from the good old days when I was a very involved member of "Team Tiger."

I am most grateful to my dear friend Earl Woods, Tiger's father. Earl has always been supportive of me, and I love him for that. I find it quite amusing that Earl signed off on the foreword to this book before the 2000 PGA Championship. Of course, Tiger went on to win that PGA in dramatic fashion, beating Bob May in a three-hole playoff at Valhalla Golf Club in Louisville, Kentucky. It should be known that, by virtue of this victory, Tiger joined Ben Hogan as the only other golfer to win three major championships in one year.

Earl's wife Tida has also been wonderful to me, and I thank her for bringing Tiger for lessons when he was just starting out. We all learned a lot of valuable lessons. Also, I will never forget the "Team Tiger" shirt she gave me, honoring my commitment to her son.

I also thank Dr. Jay Brunza, who taught me so much about the mental side of golf. During the years I taught Tiger, Jay would always find out what we were working on. Then, using his skills in psychology, he'd help Tiger understand my concepts intellectually. Further, he would encourage Tiger to use positive imagery to swing according to my instructions and hit creative shots.

Last, but certainly not least, I thank my wife, Janet, and also my two children, Danny and Rona, for their support.

# INTRODUCTION

I will never forget the spring of 1986. That was the year a California-based golf professional, Ray Oakes, called me to arrange a meeting between Earl Woods and me. Ray got right to the point, informing me that Earl was interested in having me teach Tiger the finer points of the game. Well, I had known all about Tiger's incredible track record as a golfer. After all, on a regular basis, his name was all over the sports pages.

Shortly after Ray's telephone call I met with Earl for a rather lengthy meeting, where we discussed my teaching philosophy. I'm happy to say that at the end of the meeting I was officially made a member of "Team Tiger." Two weeks later I met ten-year-old Tiger at the Los Alamitos Golf Course in Cypress, California.

From the time Tiger and I got together on the lesson tee, we clicked and began building a bond of trust. More important, I knew I had a serious student on my hands—a ten-year-old who had a thirst for learning, a love for practice, and an obsession for doing whatever it would take to become the best player in the world.

As our lessons continued I could see that Tiger was no ordinary student. He learned the vital elements of the swing very quickly owing to an uncanny

Jack Nicklaus (right) has always been Tiger's idol.

ability to absorb my tips intellectually and then physically apply them to the letter. On the negative side he seemed to be growing taller every day. That was a problem, particularly during Tiger's early teenage years, because he had to constantly change his swing plane from flat to more upright. This meant that Tiger had to get used to setting up closer to the ball with his hands closer to his body. Even though he made those adjustments, he still had to get rid of the habit of making a rounded action and swinging the club behind his body on the backswing. I instructed Tiger to move the club straight back initially along the target line, going back then upward with the club staying in front of him. Although Tiger felt uncomfortable swinging in this fashion, he was encouraged to practice this movement when I told him what Jack Nicklaus, his idol, said about the upright swing in his book, *Golf My Way.*

"An upright plane gives the golfer his best chance of swinging the club along the target line at impact," wrote Nicklaus.

Although Tiger's father and Rudy Duran had done an excellent job of teaching Tiger before he began working with me, I still had to make minor adjustments to his setup and fix a main problem in his swing. Tiger's rhythm lacked consistency. Sometimes he swung too fast and on too flat a plane, and thus had trouble coordinating the movement of the club with the movement of his body. When these faults occur it's difficult to return the center of the clubface into the center of the ball at impact consistently, which is an even bigger problem if you want to evolve into the world's top golfer. Successful professionals, even short hitters, hit the ball on the fairway when driving and onto the green when hitting an approach. And when they do miss their target, they are only a little off so they can usually save par quite easily. In Tiger's case, his bad shot was an uncontrollable duck hook that darted left and found such deep trouble that it caused him to shoot a bad score on a hole once or twice too often during a round. In match play you can afford to make these types of mistakes and recover, but in medal play, when the low total score wins, you surely cannot. I explained this to Tiger.

Tiger was eager to learn. The thing was, he had such a unique ability to learn a new shot-making technique quickly that I found myself teaching him a new shot almost every time he took a playing lesson. In *"A-Game" Golf,* I will teach you these same shots and others I have taught to Tiger and my other students.

I tried to keep each lesson interesting. For example, to help Tiger improve technique and smooth out his extra-quick tempo and rhythm, I asked him to look at photographs and a video of Sam Snead, since Snead had what is regarded by experts to be the most syrupy swing of any past or present golf professional. I also kept Tiger busy doing drills. Drills, such as the Basket Swing, helped Tiger (and can help you, too) feel and groove the proper technique.

Lessons related to the setup and swing, plus shot-making techniques, were important to Tiger, but those were not the only subjects we covered, as you will discover when you read *"A-Game" Golf.*

Over the several years that I taught Tiger, at the lesson tee and on the course, we devoted a tremendous amount of time to the short game, namely pitching and chipping. After all, in order to become a low-scorer you must be able to hit a variety of shots from around the green including a short pitch from light rough, running chip, lofted chip, and short and long sand shots. The list goes on, and as I told Tiger, everything becomes trickier when the lie becomes more severe and you have less than, say, twenty feet of green to work with.

Tiger wanted so much to play to pro standards that we also talked about good practice habits and the secrets to smart on-course strategy. Consequently, these areas will also be covered in *"A-Game" Golf.*

From reading this short review of my teacher-student relationship with Tiger, I think one thing is clear: we did not talk just about swing technique. That's because I am not a believer in constantly filling a player's brain with sundry swing thoughts. It's true what good instructors and good players say: "Thinking too much about technique leads to paralysis by analysis."

In *"A-Game" Golf,* I am going to take you on a journey of learning, one that promises to be far-reaching. I will walk you through the setup, teach you the most important elements of the backswing and downswing, educate you on creative shot-making, tell you how to play by the rules and according to the laws of etiquette, and give you instructions on how to fix faults in your swing. And, if you are a parent, provide you with a roadmap for giving your child a solid playing lesson.

While learning golf, have fun, trust your instincts, stay patient, study hard, and do your homework. Follow this advice and I guarantee that you will become a more proficient player or be better able to teach your child the game so many of us love.

—John Anselmo

# COAUTHOR'S
# COMMENTARY

According to the National Golf Foundation there are eight million junior golfers in America from the ages of five to seventeen. According to golf's aficionados, they all want to be the next Tiger Woods. That's certainly no surprise considering Woods' huge success as an amateur, highlighted by three successive U.S. Amateur championships, and as a pro, with his five major championship wins—the 1997 Masters, 1999 PGA, 2000 U.S. Open, 2000 British Open, and 2000 PGA. Another thing that excites junior golfers (and adults) is watching Tiger on television, a vehicle that allows him to boost his image through the creative advertising campaigns of Nike and Buick. Further, Woods is a chief ambassador for junior golf, and that makes him even more popular among young boys and girls. For them, Woods is the perfect role model. Not only is he a master swinger and shot-maker, he is a true professional familiar with rules, etiquette, and sportsmanship.

It has been well documented that Woods' father Earl played a major role in his early development. What has not been widely publicized is the fact that one other man, golf instructor John Anselmo, had a big influence on Tiger's game.

John Anselmo and Tiger celebrating two of Tiger's prestigious wins as an amateur—the 1993 USGA Junior (left) and the 1994 U.S. Amateur (right).

In the spring of 1986, Anselmo began teaching ten-year-old Tiger at the Los Alamitos Golf Course in Cypress, California. A year later he started giving Tiger lessons at Meadowlark Golf Course in Huntington Beach, California, where he still teaches full-time today, and at the nearby Navy Golf Course. In a period of eight years Anselmo gave Tiger around three hundred and fifty lessons and played about twenty-five rounds with him. He is the one man who groomed Tiger's shot-making game and helped make him the great player he is today. Both Earl Woods and Tiger Woods admit that. For this reason I find it shocking, rather inexcusable, that both GOLF Magazine and GOLF DIGEST left Anselmo off their most current "greatest teachers" list. There is no question in my mind that John Anselmo should be ranked Number One.

During the time Anselmo taught Tiger, I was deeply involved in the professional golf scene owing to my senior editor of instruction position at *GOLF Magazine*. However, I had never heard about Anselmo until I read *Training A Tiger* by Earl Woods, Tiger's father and first teacher. In the book, published in 1997, Earl recounts the dilemma of trying to recruit a teacher who could take his ten-year-old son's game to the next level and talks about how he found Anselmo, the very low-key but knowledgeable instructor.

"Through the years I had developed contacts and established relationships with numerous PGA teaching professionals at the top country clubs in Southern California," wrote Earl in the aforesaid book.

"This was made possible by Tiger's participation in the Southern California Junior Golf Association tournaments hosted by these clubs' respective head professionals. I contacted each one that I could think of and explained the situation. They all knew Tiger and his proficiency, and one name came up as the first choice: John Anselmo."

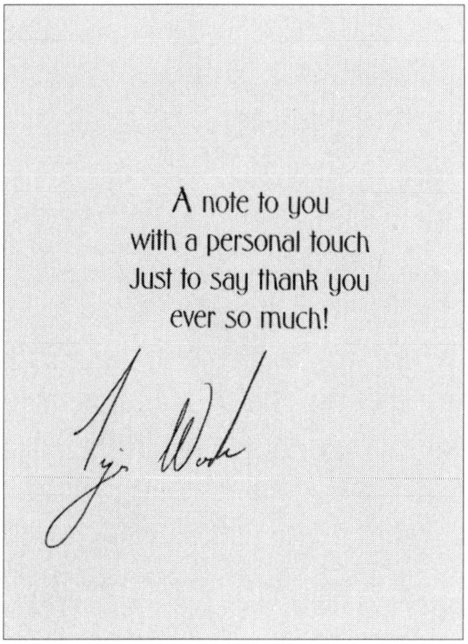

A note to you
with a personal touch
Just to say thank you
ever so much!

*Tiger Woods*

The Thank You card Tiger Woods sent Anselmo after he won the 1994 U.S. Amateur.

As you know from reading the foreword of the book you now hold in your hands, the John Anselmo–Tiger Woods relationship worked out real well. What you don't know is that Anselmo is a modest man who prefers to stay in the shadows rather than be in the limelight. Anselmo has given approximately one hundred thousand golf lessons and his students have won over two hundred tournaments. Still, Anselmo is not one to brag even though his home is filled with mementos marking Tiger's success in golf, like the Thank You card he received after Tiger won his first U.S. Amateur in 1994.

I met Anselmo for the first time in 1998, and as I watched and listened to him teach I knew right away that he was in a league of his own. One of his assets that I discovered when he gave me a lesson was a "great eye." He was able to pinpoint a fault in my swing that no other teacher had spotted and soon turned my driving game around, helping me hit the ball more powerfully and accurately.

In taking lessons from Anselmo, images of building blocks, a backyard swing, my first bicycle, and skimming stones across the water came to mind. The reason: Anselmo uses simple images and creative phraseology to communicate the most vital instructional messages. This is very refreshing and rewarding, particularly when you consider that many of today's teachers confuse students. The typical instructor is so scientific in his or her approach that the student walks away from a lesson feeling frustrated, angry, discouraged, and downright lost.

Since our first meeting I have spoken to some of Anselmo's students, many of them juniors, and learned even more about this man's methods.

Anselmo makes taking lessons fun. He breaks the swing down into simple components anyone can understand. Anselmo is also big on strengthening and stretching golf muscles since this training expedites the learning process, allows children to repeat a good swing, and provides them with the controlled power they need to play better golf. When teaching Tiger, Anselmo put him on a regular drill exercise program.

Anselmo also teaches according to his own set of basics that involve such innovative technical points as flexing the hips and knees. After teaching students a set of unique fundamentals that apply to the address and the swing, he takes them out on the course. But rather than devote time and energy to the swing itself, Anselmo teaches students how to hit a variety of shots they will inevitably be confronted with during a round.

"Many of today's golf coaches are so concerned with teaching young players to develop a mechanically perfect, pretty swing that they forget about teaching players how to shoot lower scores and lower their handicap through inventive shot-making," says Anselmo.

During a playing lesson, Anselmo shows students what adjustments need to be made in order to hit balls off an uphill lie, out of deep rough, off of hardpan . . . you name it. Anselmo's playing lessons are so informative that he guarantees he can get young players to chop strokes off their scores just by giving them good advice on course strategy and shot-making management.

In teaching students how to hit shots, Anselmo uses a unique approach that revolves around feel and imagery. For example, in teaching how to explode the ball out of sand, Anselmo instructs students to feel the sand's texture through the feet, and then cut out a certain amount of sand depending on whether the sand is soft, extra-soft, or firm. Anselmo actually has students stare intently at the sand until they confirm that they have visualized the size and depth of the sand to be removed from the bunker. Before the swing, Anselmo has the student imagine the ball riding atop the cutting of sand, as if on a magic carpet. This imagery makes the shot fun for the child—and the adult—and allows the student to make a pressure-free swing.

Something even more special about Anselmo is his ability to communicate with children on their level. He is the opposite of the pushy parent who puts pressure on a child. Anselmo has his own ways of turning juniors into champions.

Anselmo is deeply involved with high school golf teams, junior tournaments, the American Junior Golf Association, and college scholarship candidates. Moreover, he has a knack for helping children improve at a rapid pace. Figuratively and literally, he puts his arm around each student and encourages them to have fun. And in doing so he provides a solid foundation for the child to want to improve in a tension-free atmosphere. Anselmo is a father figure and friend who children feel comfortable talking to.

Anselmo's ability to allow children to get rid of their emotional baggage, through intimate talks with him, is a great asset. However, when it comes to expressing emotion on the course, Anselmo does not tolerate a student over-reacting. He encourages each player to try to stay on an even keel, whether they score a birdie or double bogey on a hole. He also stresses the one-shot-at-a-time philosophy and will not tolerate excuses. The reason for his tough-ness: his ultimate goal is to take young golfers and turn them into champions, so that they win golf scholarships or turn pro one day.

When your child reads "A-Game" Golf, they will have no excuse for not improving and will feel that they are right there on the lesson tee or out on the course, being tutored by Anselmo—and not just on the basics of the setup and swing.

"A-Game" Golf covers a wide range of topics. Tiger's former teacher will educate readers on choosing the right equipment, playing according to the rules and the laws of etiquette, keeping the body in good shape, good practice habits, creative shot-making, course management, and much more. And Anselmo knows what he's talking about. He once chipped in a record five times during a round and has scored eleven hole-in-ones during his lifetime.

Good luck in your quest to teach your children the same techniques that helped Tiger grow into a champion, and in using Anselmo's tips to lower your own handicap.

—John Andrisani

# MY LIFE
# IN GOLF

## A PASSION FOR THE GAME IS A LINK

## TO IMPROVEMENT

**T**here is nothing I like more than teaching golf under the bright sunshine or a shady tree. I get excited being involved in the give-and-take relationship with a student—be it a junior, young adult, or senior player. What I enjoy most is taking on the challenge of trying to help a student learn the game from scratch. Of course, too, I get a kick when a more experienced student improves their existing swing to such a degree that they learn to play a variety of new shots while lowering their handicap and enjoying the game more in the process.

My passion for golf began early on in my life. Born in 1921, by the time I reached the age of eleven I was hitting balls at a driving range, luckily built across the street from my original home in West Los Angeles.

To earn pocket money I picked up balls from the range using a gadget similar to the modern ball retriever, however not before I walked around the perimeter and kept swinging until all the balls were in the central part of the range. That center spot was my target. I would stare at the target for a couple of seconds, then down at the ball, then swing, letting my natural instincts take over. Focusing on a target encourages you to visualize a particular shot you intend to play. This pre-swing visual procedure, although quick time-wise, also encourages the body to find a way to swing the club into impact, with the ball getting in the way of the club's face.

## THE VALUE OF THE BASKET SWING DRILL
## AND THE BENEFITS OF CADDYING

When hitting balls to the collection area target, I used what could best be described as a pitching swing, although I swung a nine iron rather than a pitching wedge. The technique that worked best was a swing controlled by the arms. I found that when I used a compact, big, muscle-controlled action rather than a loose swing controlled by the hands and wrists, I was better able to propel the ball into the air and hit the target more consistently. To groove the arm swing, I invented the Basket Swing drill. I still remember what happened as if it were yesterday.

I simply took my address position by spreading my feet apart, balancing my weight on the ball of each foot, and letting my arms hang down naturally. But, rather than holding a club, I held a small, empty, metal driving range basket normally used to hold about fifty golf balls. I grasped the left side of the basket with the sensitive fingers of my left hand, and the right side of the basket with the fingers of my right hand. Next, I simply swung back naturally, sort of pushing the basket back away from the target while stretching the muscles in my back and left arm. Then I swung the basket toward the target. Naturally and automatically, and quite magically, the balance of my weight shifted to my right foot and leg on the backswing then onto my left foot and leg on the forward swing. I never had to think of shifting my weight or swinging through. The thrust of the arm swing carried me back and through. I had discovered the essence of a natural swinging action, controlled by my instincts. I never forgot this drill and still use it with all my new students. It is particularly good for beginners because it allows them to quickly program the proper basic actions involved in a technically correct on-balance swing into their subconscious mind. Once these elements of the swing register in the brain, the student is more likely to repeat a good action virtually automatically, not by thinking about it but by *feeling* it.

In 1933, when I turned twelve, I started caddying at the nearby Fox Hills Golf Club. I truly was in heaven there. The course featured a nice, manicured putting green and a pitching green, so after my round was finished I would practice until dark. When I wasn't practicing I would go out on the course looking for balls. I fished balls out of the woods and water hazards of this course and later Baldwin Hills, then eventually Sunset Fields Golf Course. I used to find so many balls that I kept a big supply in my home to use in practice and play. Others I sold to the golfers I caddied for to earn a little extra spending money.

In those early days, before the pro gave me a full set of clubs, I had just a seven-iron and a nine-iron. Now this may seem like a bad thing, but it was actually a good thing. Either of these clubs served me well, because by opening or closing the club, choking down or up, lightening or firming up my grip pressure, strengthening or weakening my grip, swinging more briskly or more slowly, I could hit a variety of shots. For example, to hit a running shot with the nine-iron, I simply played the ball back in my stance and let my hands lead the club's head into the ball. To hit a soft lob shot with the seven-iron, I just played the ball more forward in the stance and laid the club's face wide open. Quickly I learned that the art of shot-making depends a lot on your imagination and improvisation. I recommend that all players learn to play first with one or two clubs, preferably since great shot-makers such as Seve Ballesteros learned this way.

The secret to learning with one club is allowing your imagination to run wild. Set the ball up and down in the grass. Take square, open, and closed stances. Play the ball well forward, way back, and everywhere in between. Swing on the desired upright plane and on a flat plane, too. Swing with active hands and passive hands. Put some leg action into the shot one time, leave it out the next. Move the club on an out-to-in path and on an in-to-out path. Hit

Here one of my students, Billy Olsen, demonstrates the vital positions of the **Basket Swing Drill:** address (photograph 6), takeaway (photograph 7), top of backswing (photograph 8), downswing (photograph 9), follow-through (photograph 10), and finish (photograph 11).

6.

7.

10.

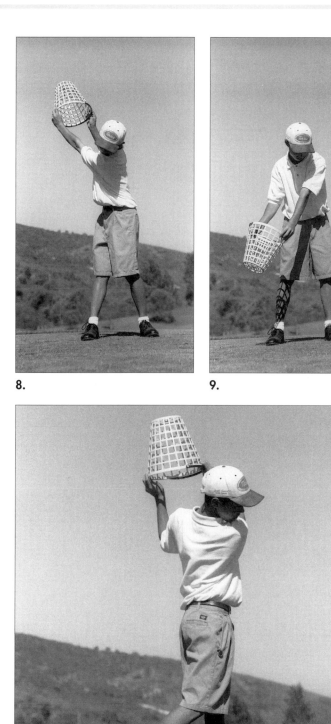

8.

9.

11.

Opening the clubface of a seven-iron, then swinging, is a good way to learn the art of shot-improvisation.

long shots, then middle distance shots, then short shots with the same club. Go with your instincts, all the time carefully watching and feeling which actions do what to the golf ball, then memorize and learn them.

Ballesteros, who learned to play with a three-iron, said he would have preferred to learn with the seven-iron—the very same club I practiced so much with as a boy and start students with. Tiger practiced hard with a seven-iron early in his life. In fact, it was the second club given to him.

The seven-iron has much more loft than the three-iron, it is two inches shorter in the shaft, and it's more upright in lie and therefore far less awkward to swing.

You are more likely to groove a more upright swing plane by learning the game with a seven-iron. I see this as a major plus-factor. The upright swing is ideal for playing many short shots. Also, the laws of physics dictate that this type of swing plane allows the club to stay closer to the target line than it does during a flat swing. Consequently, the upright swinger has the best chance of delivering the clubhead directly along the target line through impact.

Tiger and other creative players believe what I believe: *If you give this way of learning a little time, you will be pleasantly surprised at how much it helps every aspect of your golf game.*

We used to have one-club contests in the caddy yard, which I loved because they taught me to get used to playing under pressure and to improvise when playing shots. I loved the caddy-scene, particularly carrying a bag on the course, because there I got to watch good players and bad players. The low-handicap players taught me things, as did the less talented players. No matter what caliber of player I caddied for, I closely analyzed their swing and tried to determine what made (or did not make) their technique tick. Because I caddied for so many different men and women, I knew what subtleties of the swing worked better for short players, tall players, players of medium stature, heavy players, skinny players, ones with small hands, big hands, flexible and less agile players, stronger and weaker players.

I loved the education that caddying provided. I met individuals from all walks of life, and I got to play the course for free or at a low price with friends. I played my first round at Sunset Fields, with the set of clubs I had saved up enough money to buy. I shot 94 and realized that golf was not as easy as it looks. There is a world of difference between hitting balls on the driving range and playing on the course. The main reason is, on the range you are not playing for score. On the course you are required to hit the ball in between rows of trees and avoid hazards that lurk between the area of the tee and the area of the green. If you miss the "short grass," you must hit a good recovery shot and putt well to shoot a reasonably good score. Pressure enters the picture more on the course than in practice, especially on the green. Playing my first round, I realized right away that the pressure to hole out is much more intense on the course than in practice, when you have a more casual attitude.

I caddied during the summers of my school years, all the time working on my game. I played and practiced so much that I got my handicap down to scratch, and by the time I was eighteen years old I had even broken par several times. I knew then that I wanted to play golf for a living. But fate was not going to work in my favor just yet.

My life in golf stopped when World War II broke out. At the time I was also training as a gymnast for the Olympics. However, as you can understand, that sport also had to take a backseat to the call of duty and serving my country. I joined the service when I turned twenty-one and stayed active until 1946.

## LEARNING FROM GOLF'S GREATEST PLAYERS

When I got out of the service my game was rusty. I had not lifted a club for several years, but I was anxious to play. I practiced very hard to retrieve my good game and the work paid off. A year later, in 1947, I turned professional and began playing the circuit among the likes of Ben Hogan and Sam Snead. I was not as good as these players, but I sure learned a lot about the swing and shot-making from these two golfing lions.

What I enjoyed most about these two players were their contrasting styles. Snead was taller and more flexible than Hogan, worked his feet very actively, made a stronger body coil, employed a relaxed type swing, and normally hit a right to left draw shot. When Snead took his address position, the good balance and grace he possessed became instantly obvious. Further, his smooth way of waggling the club back and forth was a harbinger of the poetic swing to come. Snead gave the impression that his body was free of any tension, loose as a goose, that he was feeling more than thinking.

In setting up to play the draw off the tee, Snead teed the ball up high. This raised tee position promotes a flat arc of swing, which in turn allows the hands and forearms to rotate more in a counterclockwise direction through impact. These rolling-over actions also make the clubhead rotate more—toe leading the heel—which is basically how heavy right to left overspin is imparted on the ball.

To further encourage a slightly flatter swing plane, Snead strengthened his left hand grip by turning his hand a tad clockwise, until the V formed by the thumb and forefinger pointed to his right shoulder when the driver was placed behind the ball. When Snead's club rested on the ground at address, its face pointed right of target. This was the line he wanted the ball to start its flight on.

Many of the natural elements of John Anselmo's swing, shown here, mirror what he learned from Sam Snead and Ben Hogan.

To promote a very active and free and natural turn of the right hip on the backswing, Snead set his right foot back a couple of inches farther from the target line than his left foot, in what is commonly called a *closed* position. This stance also helped him swing the club back on a flatter plane.

Since Snead wanted to extend the club back low and inside the target line, to promote a powerful arc on the backswing he assumed a wide stance. Standing with the feet too close together causes you to pick up the club too quickly in the takeaway, which narrows your swing arc and thus ultimately cuts off power.

Snead had a tremendously big windup. His shoulders and hips turned to the max.

Once Snead reached the top of the swing, he uncoiled his right hip, which pushed his weight back over to his left side and caused his knees to first square up to the target, then rotate toward it. Both of these movements helped Snead regain his balance and ready himself for the hit. Releasing his right side toward the target also helped him clear his left hip more easily. Once that clearing action was triggered, the arms extended out at the ball. At this point in Snead's swing, it was almost as if I could see and feel the building pulse of power being transmitted through his arms and hands.

When Snead's hands dropped to a level even with his thighs, his right forearm started rotating in a counterclockwise direction. The instant this rotation began, multiplying power started transferring down the clubshaft into the clubhead. Then, once he released his hands with the final, delayed uncocking of the wrists, the clubhead was whipped into the ball while the face started to close, thereby creating draw-flight and powerful overspin.

Hogan, whose bread-and-butter shot was a controlled fade, gave one the impression that he was tense and perhaps overthinking. Hogan was several inches shorter than Snead but more muscular. His left foot stayed flat on the ground, his shoulder turn was not as full as Snead's, and his swing was more mechanical. You could tell by looking at Hogan that he had worked hard to develop his swing, whereas Snead seemed to be a born-golfer. One thing is certain though, Hogan's swing repeated itself over and over again, which is the essence of a good technique.

Hogan set up differently than Snead. He set his hands behind the ball slightly, since this position he knew would promote a wide takeaway but, more important, prevent an overly rounded backswing. He avoided that at all costs, for fear of hitting a duck hook. Hogan also believed that the more resistance there was between the upper and lower body, the more torque generated in the swing, the more powerful the swing. In short, he wanted the shoulders to turn more than the hips. He put a governor on his hip turn by pointing the toe-end of his right foot perpendicular to the target line, whereas Snead pointed it outward. Snead's position is much more natural, and one that Tiger prefers because it gives him a sense of freedom from the ground up.

To promote a fade, Hogan used a weak grip, setting his hands more on top of the club, with the Vs pointing directly up at his chin.

Hogan's backswing was very compact, whereas Snead's was long. Most modern-day players, including Tiger Woods, employ a slightly shorter swing simply because they feel it enhances their control. When you swing the club beyond the parallel position (clubshaft parallel to the target line at the top of the swing), you run the risk of overhinging the wrists. In turn, this faulty position tends to cause you to release the club too early and hit a weak, off-line shot.

In swinging down, Hogan first shifted his hips laterally, to give his arms a chance to catch up with his lower body, then he cleared his hips in a counterclockwise direction. The lateral movement of Hogan's hips also helped him delay the unhinging of the wrists, one of his secrets to power. In the hitting area, he held on more firmly with his left hand to hold the clubface slightly open at impact, which ensured a powerful left-to-right fade shot.

I think you can appreciate that there are technical aspects about the swings of both Snead and Hogan that I like. In fact, in teaching my present students (and previously Tiger) I use both of these players as models, although I admit to liking Snead's technique and naturalness more than Hogan's mechanical action.

The advantage of playing golf around players such as Hogan and Snead was that they helped educate me on the qualities of being a top-notch golfer. Snead taught me that you should never force the swing, but rather swing the force— the golf club. Snead simply let the swing happen. In other words, he perfectly coordinated the movement of the golf club with the movement of the body. This is opposite to the average high-handicap players who fail to move these two forces rhythmically in unison. Rather, they pull the club on an exaggerated flat path on the backswing, or push it well outward. As Snead taught me, the club should move straight back, then slightly inside as the shoulders turn.

Snead is thought of by experts to have the best swing ever, and I agree. The reason he looked so smooth yet generated such high clubhead speed and hit the ball powerfully was because he made a flowing transition into the downswing. High-handicappers tend to jut the right shoulder outward at the start of the downswing, for the simple reason that they work the club well behind their body on the backswing—into an area that I'd like you to imagine as being marked by a "Keep Out" sign.

Snead learned the game through trial and error and by watching his brother Homer hit balls across the back pasture of their Virginia family farm. When you teach yourself golf, you take a real inventory of what your body is doing at all times. And that check-system allows you to swing the club almost entirely by feel. I think every golfer should spend a little time learning on their own before they book a lesson with a qualified teacher. This way, you at least give yourself time to build a personal swing based on your innate strengths and weaknesses, natural tendencies, and flexibility. So by the time a teacher sees you, he knows right away what you can and cannot do, which allows him to more easily tweak your action in his own way, as I did with Tiger.

Another thing that made Snead great was that, when swinging the club, he used only about 80 percent of the power available to him. He "swung within himself," which is what we teachers like to say. Snead also concentrated on trying to finish high, knowing if he had that goal in mind he would not get hung up on the process of hitting the ball. When you try to hit at the ball, the tendency is to hit behind it or across it. Thinking of finishing high will encourage you to make square and solid contact with the ball at impact.

Speaking of solid contact, there were a couple of reasons why Snead hit the ball so powerfully and accurately. He liked to feel oily, which is a key that will help you make a tension-free swing. He also never got hung up in swing thoughts. Instead, he played largely by feel, which is something I have always encouraged Tiger and other players to do. I suggest that, every single time you practice, try and feel the movements of the body and club during the swing, so you are better able to repeat that action over and over again—just like Hogan did.

When discussing the attributes of Hogan's technique with students, I eagerly point out how solid his setup was. You need this strong foundation if you intend to make a fluid, on-balance swing. What I liked most about Hogan's address was his posture. He bent over comfortably and correctly from the ball-and-socket joints of the hips while keeping the knees relatively straight, but not locked. As he bent to the ball, he let his buttocks extend out a bit to counterbalance the weight of the upper body. This position allowed Hogan to set his weight more into the hips, rather than the knees.

By keeping the legs straighter and bending more from the hips, Hogan created a sharper angle between the legs and the spine—it should be about thirty degrees. This position ensures that you stand the right distance from the ball and also enables the body to turn more freely going back and coming down into the ball. It creates the proper angle of address at which 95 percent of all the work in the golf swing is done.

Another aspect of Hogan's technique that I have never heard talked about is the way he used to stay in motion from the time he stepped into the shot to the time he finished the swing. There was no stop-start aspect of Hogan's swing. His back and forth waggling action of the club seemed to grow out of his setup and lead him right into the takeaway. When he reached the top of the swing, there was no pause either. The lateral action of Hogan's hips helped him move smoothly into impact, then through into the finish. I really impressed these assets of Hogan's onto Tiger, and it shows. His swing is always smooth, never choppy.

## MY TEACHING CAREER TAKES OFF

Playing the professional circuit was great fun and I learned a lot about the swing and shot-making. I liked this life so much that I moved my family to Carmel, the golf Mecca of the United States, and began playing in Monday pro-am events at some of the world's very top courses such as Pebble Beach, Cypress Point, and San Francisco Golf Club. What a great golf experience it was playing these fantastic courses. The more I played them the better I got, simply because these courses encourage you to hit creative shots. Again, however, the hand of fate was at work.

Kim Saiki, who started taking lessons from Anselmo at age eleven, is now an LPGA player. However, she enjoyed great success as an amateur, as evidenced by the 1987 USGA Junior and 1987 World Junior trophies she earned.

My professional tournament golf days ended in 1950, when a ball hit by a player on the driving range struck me above the left eye. I spent two weeks in the hospital and the doctors thought I was going to lose sight in the eye. Fortunately I did not, but the injury did hurt my depth perception. Consequently, I moved to Long Beach, California, and started teaching.

I held teaching positions at Lakewood Golf Course, Antelope Valley Country Club, Royal Palms Golf Course, and Mile Square Golf Course in Fountain Valley in 1976. It was there that I met eleven-year-old Kim Saiki. She planned to play on the golf team at Ocean View High and her father suggested that she take professional lessons. Saiki proved to be one of my top students, as evidenced by her success as an amateur and as a pro on the LPGA Tour.

In 1986, I was based at the Los Alamitos Golf Course in Cypress, California, not far from where Tiger lived. Los Alamitos is now called Cypress Golf Course.

As I said in the introduction to this book, in early 1986 a fellow professional, Ray Oakes, set up a meeting for me with Tiger's father Earl. Two weeks after Earl and I spoke in person, Tiger showed up for a lesson at Los Alamitos. I began teaching Tiger there about once a week. A year later I moved to Meadowlark Golf Course, where I maintained the same type of schedule with Tiger, although sometimes we worked together at the nearby Navy Golf Course.

I still teach golf at Meadowlark today. I still love it and, honestly, as has always been the case, I continue to learn something new every day. Before getting into a detailed account of my experiences with Tiger, I want to talk to you about some of the myths of the golf swing so you can avoid making errors early on in the learning process.

## Address Myths

### SET THE HANDS SLIGHTLY AHEAD OF THE BALL

I guess I must be a rebel because I believe it's better to set the hands slightly behind the ball when hitting the longer clubs, particularly a driver. Tiger does, as did Hogan and Snead before him. This address position encourages you to drag the club away low to the ground in the initial stage of the backswing rather than pick it up, and promotes the natural, elongated pitch-type swing I recommend. Snead also had fought a hook, but one not as severe as Hogan's, so he set his hands only slightly behind the ball. Hogan, in contrast, set his hands about two to three inches behind the ball.

### SET THE RIGHT FOOT PERPENDICULAR TO THE TARGET LINE

Before Hogan wrote his most popular book, *Five Lessons,* I had never heard a golf professional teach this foot position to students. However, once the book came out in 1957, and Hogan the master ball-striker talked about it, practically every teacher I knew started recommending that golfers do what Hogan did. I have nothing against a player standing this way, provided that they have a problem over-turning the hips and need to restrict this action. I certainly would not call this position a basic or fundamental. I prefer to have the student stand naturally to the ball, like Tiger does, with both feet splayed outward—the left foot more than the right.

### LOOK AT THE BACK OF THE BALL

When setting up to drive, look through the ball positioned in front of your eyes rather than at the back of it, as this encourages you to make a fluid action through impact. Staring at the back portion of the ball encourages you to hit it with a glancing blow.

## Backswing Myths

### KEEP THE LEFT ARM STIFF

You never want the left arm to be stiff or tense, or you will cheat yourself out of vital club speed due to a robot-like swinging action. Many top-notch professionals such as Fred Couples, David Duval, and Phil Mickelson allow the left arm to bend slightly on the backswing, and they are all superb ball-strikers. Nevertheless, do not allow the left arm to be limp because its major purpose is to guide the club back and through in the ball area. For the best results allow the left arm to stretch comfortably during the backswing.

### SET THE CLUB IN THE SLOT, WITH ITS SHAFT PARALLEL TO THE TARGET LINE

Modern-day PGA Tour pros—everybody from Tiger Woods to David Duval to Davis Love—prove that this fundamental is not true at all. All three of these players make a much more compact swing.

Here, student Robert Kramer proves that good players can set the hands behind the ball at address, splay the right foot outward, and look through the ball rather than at the back of it.

Many amateurs are under the impression that the longer the swing, the more power will be generated with a more powerful impact of club to ball. I always believed there was no truth to that theory, and a couple of years ago a team of scientists proved me right. Ironically, many players generate more clubhead speed and hit the ball longer off the tee using a short swing, providing that the arc of their swing is wide.

## TURN THE SHOULDERS NINETY DEGREES, THE HIPS FORTY-FIVE DEGREES

It is ridiculous to think that players should be expected to think of angles, as if they each had a protractor in their hip pocket when swinging the club. Too many teachers who instruct students to heed the above instructions turn a simple game into rocket science.

It's perfectly okay to swing the driver short of parallel, and to let the left arm bend slightly on the backswing.

Some professionals make a stronger coiling action of the body, while others make a weaker turn than what is too often referred to as the classic 90-45 shoulder-to-hip combination. However, both types of swingers hit the ball long or long enough.

I do not tell my students to think of turning their body and I certainly do not measure their angles. I want them to plane the shoulders by working their back muscles properly and flex the hips rather than turn them. I also want students to think of making a throwing motion, where they ready themselves to make an on-balance throw on the backswing, then throw the club toward the target (just as they do the basket in the Basket Swing drill) while still holding onto it. In short, the shifting action, as teachers and students know it, happens automatically. It is not a conscious action.

## Downswing Myths

### DRIVE THE LEGS TOWARD THE TARGET

For some reason, during the early 1960s many golf teachers started talking about Jack Nicklaus's great leg drive. Consequently, many instructors started telling students to drive their legs toward the target at the start of the downswing. This is the worst thing you can do, namely because it causes you to get so far out ahead of the ball that the club lags far behind. As a result you leave the clubface well open at impact and hit a push or push-slice shot right of target.

To me there is no such thing as leg drive. Granted, it does look like the right leg drives through the ball. But this is a misconception. If you drive off the right leg and foot too soon, you will fail to make solid contact. In actuality, the legs actually help you swing the club through the ball, but you are not required to push or drive them toward the target. If you just think about throwing the club to the target, as in the pitching swing, the legs and feet will control the balance and equilibrium of the swing.

### UNCOIL THE HIPS AND SHOULDERS

From my experience, golfers who are told to consciously make an uncoiling action of the body land themselves in trouble. Typically, once most players reach the top of the swing, they vigorously turn the hips in a counterclockwise direction. When you exaggerate hip action in this fashion (or try to consciously uncoil the shoulders), you tend to pull the club across the target line through impact instead of swinging it down the line.

It only takes about one-fifth of a second to swing down to the ball from the top, so no player has any business trying to make a conscious effort to unwind the hips and shoulders. Again, if you just keep the hands quiet and let the arms swing the club toward the target, you will automatically unwind both

Swinging through the ball and toward the target is what's important, not swinging out "at" the ball.

the hips and shoulders. If the timing of your swing is good, the hips and shoulders will face the target line before impact and for a moment match the position they were in when you took your address. The left shoulder will be higher than the right shoulder—in what I call a *planed position.*

Hogan, I believe, made a big mistake when describing his lower body action in his book *Five Lessons.* In writing about the downswing, he mentioned that the faster the uncoiling action of the hips, the more power is generated. Hogan claimed that he unwound the hips at the start of the downswing when, in fact, his hips moved laterally toward the target first. Sadly, the millions of golfers who have read this book and continue to read it today have been misinformed. As a result they fail to return the clubface to the ball at impact and hit some kind of bad shot, usually a pull-slice that starts left of target and finishes well right of it.

## SWING OUT AT THE BALL

This advice will sure cure an over-the-top problem—swinging from out-to-in and across the ball—but it will definitely promote another problem, namely an exaggerated block-shot hit well right of target.

If you pretend you are swinging a range-ball basket, the club will naturally move along an inside path on the backswing and remain square to the target line. On the downswing the club will simply drop onto an even shallower plane, making it quite easy to return it square to the ball (clubface pointing directly at the target at impact)—that is, provided you just let the controlled thrust of the throwing action deliver the club into the ball, then through it.

You should never think about swinging out at the ball. If you do, you'll probably swing the club away from the target. The clubface should remain square and extend straight through the ball to the target.

# TEACHING TIGER

**2**

MEMORIES OF TIMES PAST,
TEACHING THE NATURAL MOTION,
AND DEALING WITH THE DIFFICULT
TASK OF MAKING A GREAT PLAYER
EVEN GREATER

In the spring of 1986, when Tiger visited Los Alamitos Golf Course for his first golf lesson, I knew as he stood before me that I had a tremendous challenge on my hands, compared perhaps to climbing Mount Everest. And I'm not exaggerating. This skinny, ten-year-old kid had already built up a reputation for being a world-beater in the junior ranks, so how was I going to help him raise the level of his game to an even higher level? That, as they say, was the $64,000 question.

As I pondered the answer to this question, I decided that I would follow one course and one course only. I promised myself that I would stick to my proven method of teaching golf, take things one step at a time, and keep everything simple. This philosophy, I knew, had always worked, so I figured why change, and start confusing Tiger by going into detail about complex plane angles, degrees of body turn, and the differences between and upper and lower body shift. Too many of today's instructors teach people golf as if they were teaching physics. Consequently, many students become discouraged, others revert back to their old bad habits, and still others actually quit the game. Some players hang tough, but to no avail. Forced into adopting an unorthodox and unproven methodology that requires many technical changes to their

When Tiger first came to Anselmo for lessons, he was already used to being in the winner's circle. Anselmo's goal was to make him an even better player.

existing motion, their swing loses any natural rhythm it had. Consequently, they lose the feel for the club and the shot they are trying to hit. I certainly did not want this to happen to Tiger, who was already a very natural player. Don't misunderstand me, once I saw Tiger swing I knew that I would have to make minor changes, but I would proceed with caution because in golf, like life, we all know that you cannot make changes overnight and get good results.

Everyone has the same instincts and reflexes, so essentially everyone is born to play golf. Furthermore, the golf swing is a pitching sense (developed via the Basket Swing drill) used to direct the club through the ball to the target. There is no such thing as muscle memory. Your mind is in your head, not in your muscles. I use the term muscle sense rather than muscle memory and tell students that I am not going to change their swing, but the way they feel through the vehicle of learning about the muscles and how the joints of the body work.

Some individuals have more muscle sense and quicker reflexes than others, which explains why the speed of swing varies among players. For example,

Here, Anselmo shows how the flexing actions of the knees play a big role in the backswing (left) and downswing (right). Practicing these flex-actions trains you to feel the parallel between the walking sensation and swinging sensation.

baseball hitters who use their hands and wrists usually swing the golf club too fast. If a male junior player who is also a baseball player visits me for lessons, and he is serious about becoming a top amateur golfer or turning professional one day, I have him swing the basket to take his hands out of the swing. I did this with Tiger, and recommended that he not play baseball, even though it was and still is America's national pastime. After the student swings the basket back and forth to loosen their back and arm muscles, I tell them to focus on a target. Without fail, they then naturally swing the basket back to their right side, staying balanced and using their arms instead of their hands to control the action, then to their left side doing the same.

In priming Tiger, I also got him to understand that the natural body movements involved in walking are essentially the same as in the golf swing, as Sam

Snead and other great players have proved. If you don't believe me, walk in place, flexing your ankles, knees, and hips. You will see that the tempo and rhythm of your swinging arms matches that of your legs. To further prove my theory, assume your golf swing posture of sitting back and bending from the ball-and-socket joints of the hips and flexing your knees. Next, unhinge your right knee until it nearly straightens. See how your hands, arms, and torso start to move automatically.

Why is the first half of the swing called the backswing, and not a hand swing or an arm swing? The answer: Your back muscles create the backward motion after being triggered by the backward flexing action of the right knee. Your feet and legs help you maintain balance and keep your upper body centered as the back muscles stretch and expand. As I explained to Tiger, the golf swing is started from the ground up. Using your right foot and leg as the balance point on the backswing motivates the upper body, arms, shoulders, and hands. Your feet, ankles, knees, and legs also control the speed of the golf club.

The muscles of the upper body simply reflex forward automatically on the forward swing. The right arm and right side provide the extension in the downswing and in the finish of the golf swing. All objects pitched, tossed, or thrown are released through the right side while balanced by the left side. This release is instinctive and directed to the muscles by the mind's reflex action. Achieving the proper release requires the correct sequence of swing reflexes: the hands must quietly set the clubface square, the left arm must be an extension of the club, and the body must control the tempo of the swing. When the swinging action of the club works in sync with the swinging action of the body, the clubhead is released naturally, with no interference or manipulation on the golfer's part.

To encourage Tiger to get acquainted with the natural swinging motion, and to prevent him from hitting at the ball, I asked him to make several practice swings to the side of the ball. To help Tiger enhance his feel for the motion of the body and appreciate just how the feet, knees, hips, and shoulders work, I asked him to shut his eyes when making a practice swing. I also had him

To help your children groove a natural swing, encourage them to practice pitching.

employ four types of pitching swings; the one-quarter swing, the half-swing pitch, the three-quarter-length swing, and the full swing.

To simplify matters, and to provide Tiger with a good checklist to study, I gave him the following quick tips:

1. The ball is incidental, and you swing through it, not at it.

2. The ball is not to be hit, but directed.

3. Don't try hard, try to be fluid.

4. Let the right hand control the face of the club.

5. Work toward feeling the swing, not thinking it out in your head.

6. Maintain the same degree of grip pressure during the swing.

7. Keep your feet active and alive during the swinging action.

8. To promote a fluid swing, allow the right wrist to be flexible.

9. Swing toward the target.

10. Hit with your practice swing.

Anselmo at the Navy Golf Course, amidst interested onlookers, teaching Tiger how to replane his swing during Tiger's growing years.

## CHANGING TIGER'S SWING PLANE

Between the years of thirteen and fifteen Tiger grew about six inches, so he was having a problem with the plane of his swing. Tiger wanted to start swinging on a more natural upright plane, but he fought this because he had an ingrained flat plane of swing better suited for short players. Consequently, I had to replane his swing and help him get rid of the bad habit of cupping his left wrist at the top, which caused the clubface to open rather than remain square. I made Tiger's swing more upright by having him stand closer to the ball and raise his hands a little higher and position them closer to his body at address. I also instructed Tiger to set his hands above his right shoulder at the completion of the backswing, rather than behind his back. So that Tiger would ingrain this vital position of the hands at the top, I had him stop at the top and "freeze" for thirty seconds, rest for thirty seconds, and repeat that same freeze-and-rest procedure until five minutes was up. After about a week Tiger got used to swinging on a more upright plane, which is the angle of swing I prefer. I think the reason Tiger caught on so quickly was not just because of his innate talent, but because of my advice to have his clubs made more upright, by about one degree. I also suggested that Tiger try playing with a driver that had a lower degree of loft, since an upright swing causes the golfer to effectively add loft to the shot when the ball is correctly hit on the upswing. A lighter grip also better allowed Tiger to make a more upright swing. Soft hands allowed him to set the club earlier in the takeaway, a characteristic common to most of today's top players.

Before talking more about the upright swing and the shots that can be played more easily with it, I will review a series of unique exercises I prescribed to Tiger. Some require a club, some do not. These fifteen exercises, like the Basket Swing drill already described, will serve as prerequisites to understanding the upright swing and the art of shot-making. They will also better enable you to train your child or improve your own game. Additionally, I will educate you, like I did Tiger, on the benefits of playing with the right equipment. Pay close attention to my tips, because only with correctly fitted clubs can you swing on-plane.

## Exercises Taught to Tiger

### LEFT HAND GRIP DRILL

The grip is the engine of the swing, namely because the hands are the only connection to the golf club. Therefore, I want to impress upon you, as I impressed upon Tiger, the vital importance of gripping the club correctly.

To train yourself to apply the correct pressure in the left hand, or "guide hand" for the backswing, practice holding the club with just the last three fingers of that hand. To gain strength in the left hand fingers, left forearm, and left wrist, freeze this position for five seconds, once a day, first while pointing the club into the air, then holding it horizontal to the ground.

### RIGHT HAND GRIP DRILL

Whereas the left hand guides the club back, the right hand helps control the clubface on the downswing and provides the power during the through-swing.

To build strength in your right hand fingers, right forearm, and right wrist, practice holding the club with the middle two fingers of your right hand. Again, freeze this position for five seconds, once a day, first while pointing the club at the sky, then holding it in a horizontal position.

### ARM SWING DRILL

Stand with your feet spread shoulder-width apart, and bend comfortably at the knees and from the ball-and-socket joints of your hips. Next, cross your arms in front of your chest. Next, grasp your left elbow with the fingers of your right hand, and your right elbow with the fingers of your left hand.

**The Arm Swing Drill:**

backswing (photo left) and downswing (photo right).

Start the backswing by rotating your right elbow away from the target.

Start the downswing by rotating your left arm toward the target, then to the left of it.

As Tiger knows, if you rotate the arms correctly you will feel the muscles in your back stretching on the way back and at the completion of the backswing and downswing. This is good because the more flexibility you gain, the more likely you are to build torque on the backswing and release it powerfully on the downswing.

## SHAFT DRILL #1

Take a shoulder-width stance and assume your normal golf swing posture. Hold the club at the butt-end of the club with your left hand so the palm of your hand presses against the shaft's end. Grasp the shaft with your right hand, about twelve inches below the bottom of the grip. When you've completed the grip, make sure you are holding the club in a horizontal position with its shaft virtually parallel to an imaginary target line.

Next, release your body toward the target, then back away from it with your left arm extended, then through with your arms staying close to your body and your feet moving in time with the swinging club. This exercise helped Tiger develop good rhythm.

**Shaft Drill #1:**

Position 1                    Position 2

Position 5

Position 3

Position 4

Position 6

**Shaft Drill #2:**

Backswing Position          Downswing Position

## SHAFT DRILL #2

Stand exactly the same way as you did for the previous exercise. Hold the club's shaft with your left hand just below the grip and your right hand close above the clubhead. Let both palms face the sky.

Swing back and through. This exercise helped Tiger, and will help you, correctly use the big muscles of the body—not the hands and wrists—to control the swinging action. It will also help you make a more natural, streamlined shoulder plane and thus prevent you from dipping the left shoulder on the backswing, the right one on the downswing. Most important, it trains you to swing on-plane during the downswing, and from inside the target line.

## THUMB AND FINGER DRILL

Take your normal address, allowing your hands and arms to hang naturally in a relaxed position. Next, grip the thumb of your left hand with the last three fingers of your right hand. Let the back of the left hand and the right palm face the target.

Swing back, then through, concentrating on keeping your arms in front of your body.

When Tiger's swing flattened and he began hitting duck hook shots, this drill helped him create a more upright swing plane and hit accurate shots.

**Thumb and Finger Drill:**

Position 1

Position 2

Position 3

### PRE-SET DRILL

Hinging the right wrist quite early in the takeaway is very critical to swinging the club back on the proper plane. The unhinging action of the right wrist on the downswing is a very important link to maintaining a square clubface position through impact, and maintaining power.

In order to feel the proper action, extend the left arm and set the right wrist back fully as you swing back, then try to delay the unhinging action until the last vital moment of the downswing.

Wait until you have gotten your timing down before you begin actually hitting balls.

### RIGHT HAND ONLY SWING DRILL

Take a natural-feeling address. Hold the club in your right hand, making sure that your right thumb is touching the grip for balance, and your fingers and right arm are relaxed. Make sure, too, that the right arm is extended comfortably downward. Next, grasp your right biceps muscle with your left hand, so that your left forearm is parallel to the target line and the back of your left hand faces it.

Swing back, feeling the natural pivot-action of the feet and body and the hinging action of the right wrist.

Swing down, concentrating on the toward-the-target pivot action, the right forearm and wrist lever, and the rhythm of weight moving through the feet.

### LEFT HAND ONLY SWING DRILL

Take a natural-feeling address. Hold the club lightly with only your left hand, a few inches from the butt-end of the club. Extend your left arm straight down. Next, grasp your left biceps and elbow with your right hand, so that your right forearm is practically parallel to the target line and the back of your right hand faces it.

Backswing Position

Downswing Position

**Right Hand
Only Drill:**

Backswing Position

Downswing Position

**Left Hand
Only Drill:**

Swing back, keeping your upper left arm close to your body.

Swing down, feeling the club being pulled toward the target.

As Tiger learned, this exercise trains you to swing the club on the proper path, so that the left arm stays "connected" to the body and the left forearm releases more naturally.

## HANDS APART DRILL

Take your driver setup, with your feet spread slightly more than shoulder-width apart. Hold the driver with your hands spread a few inches apart. Lift the club up, so that the grip-end points directly at your belt buckle or belly button and its shaft runs perpendicular to an imaginary target line.

Starting with the club elevated off the ground, swing back and then through, trying to feel the proper actions of the club and body. Through the

One of the benefits of the **Hands Apart Drill** is that it helps you stabilize your shoulder plane on the backswing.

impact zone, feel the right hand rotate over the left. Because your hands are separated, the action will be less loose. Therefore, this exercise trains you, as it did Tiger, to stabilize your swing plane and master the inside-out attack track, so you're more likely to hit a good shot.

### RIGHT FOOT AND RIGHT LEG STEP DRILL

Take your normal address posture, but keep your feet together as you set the club down.

Next, take a full step back with your right foot to create a full shoulder-width stance, while simultaneously swinging the club back to the top.

This exercise trains you to feel how your natural walking-sense allows you to swing back and pivot around a single pivot post comprised of your right foot and leg.

After setting up for the **Right Foot** and **Right Leg Step Drill** (photograph, left), step back and swing to the top (photograph, right) so that you feel your right side pivot post.

As you complete the **Left Foot** and **Left Leg Step Drill,** feel your left side pivot post.

### LEFT FOOT AND LEFT LEG STEP DRILL

Start from where you left off in the previous exercise—at the top of the swing—but with your feet together again.

Next, take a full step to the left and swing down. Feel how your natural walking-sense allows you to time the downward motion while pivoting around your left foot and leg "post."

### FOLLOW-THROUGH DRILL

Start this exercise from the halfway down position of the downswing. Next, release the club down into the follow-through, stopping when the clubshaft parallels the ground. As you swing into this position, once again feel how changing from a right foot balance to a left foot balance aids the movement of the club and your torso. Freezing this position for ten seconds will help you feel the proper right-hand-over-left position and make you more apt to arrive in this very same good position when you start hitting balls.

### MIRROR IMAGE DRILL (BACKSWING)

Face a full-length mirror (or a pane-glass window). Since the mirror is a superb teaching aid, namely because it provides instant feedback, it's fairly common to see one or two on wheels at a public driving range or at your local club's practice area.

Swing back to the top. If you made a good backswing and stretched your muscles, you should observe obvious wrinkles in your shirt from under your left shoulder down your back to your waist, and on your pants stretching from your right hip to your left knee.

When swinging back in front of a mirror (or pane-glass window), you should notice wrinkles in the same areas where they appear here on John Anselmo's clothing.

When swinging through in front of a mirror (or pane-glass window), you should notice wrinkles in the same areas as they appear here on John Anselmo's clothing.

### Mirror Image Drill (Downswing)

Stand in front of a full-length mirror (or a pane-glass window). Swing to the top and stop.

Swing down into the finish. If you employed a balanced backswing action and swung the club powerfully through, you should observe wrinkles stretching from under your right shoulder, down across the right side of your back to your right hip.

### Helpful Equipment Hints

Tiger learned with a cut-down club, as most children did until quite recently. Of course, when Tiger did get a full set, he grew so fast he grew out of them.

During his junior days he went through about five different sets, always getting his shafts lengthened even though he preferred to choke down slightly on the handle, as he still does today.

Nowadays, club manufacturers recognize the importance of catering to the younger generation. And they should. According to a recent survey conducted by the National Golf Foundation, the annual growth rate in the junior golf population has been three to four times more than the annual growth rate of the overall golf population. According to this survey, over the next seven years prospects for continued growth are especially good because of the population bulge of "echo boomers." Echo boomers are important because, like their baby boom parents before them, they will be establishing recreational preferences and brand loyalty patterns for years to come.

Manufacturers are now making custom junior clubs that feature shorter pro-fit shafts that are light in weight. These clubs are ideal for juniors age five

Nowadays, manufacturers are producing shorter clubs for young players. See for yourself the difference between the standard "metal wood" club and the shorter junior club held by Alexandra Anselmo.

If the heel of the clubhead is off the ground, the club needs to be made more upright. Your local pro can adjust the lie angle.

to nine. If your child is tall and strong and ten to twelve years old, he or she should be using longer and heavier shafts to help strengthen their muscles. The length and lie of the club should be determined by the player's height and the length of their arms. The shaft flex should be determined by the player's strength. Generally speaking, taller players with short arms should use a longer club with a more upright lie. The shorter player with long arms should use a shorter club with a less upright lie. Players who generate clubhead speed of around 85 to 100 miles per hour should swing clubs with stiff shafts. Players who swing the club at a slower speed should use more flexible shafts, probably of graphite construction.

The period of age thirteen to seventeen is usually the time when a teenager grows the most. However, age is not the only factor in fitting a student with the proper clubs. I teach some older juniors who use medium-flex shafts, while other younger players swing stiff shafts. Normally the following rule applies: the stronger the player, the stiffer the shaft. Some players, particularly young girls, prefer a graphite shaft over a steel shaft because it's lighter and thus easier to swing.

I believe the best approach is to have your child checked by the pro at your local golf course. The pro will be able to tell if the grips should be built up because the youngster has large hands and if the lie is correct just by looking at

If the toe of the clubhead is off the ground, the club needs to be flattened. Again, your local pro can adjust the lie angle.

how the club sits on the ground. If the toe is off the ground, the club needs to be made flatter. If the heel is off the ground, the player needs clubs with a more upright lie and probably should have the swing replaned to be more upright. It's important that you deal with these growing pains right away so your child will be able to employ the desired upright swing.

The upright swing is useful for playing a variety of shots—everything from a power-fade tee shot, to a fairway iron shot off a downhill slope, to a bunker shot from a buried lie. Of course, as Tiger realizes, other subtleties are involved in playing these shots, that I will review shortly. I will present them the same way I did to Tiger, by providing both a conventional method of hitting the shot along with my way of playing the same shot. I feel this is the best way to educate you, so you can make comparisons and judge for yourself which method works best for you or your child. Later on, in chapter 5, I'll discuss many more creative shots that each require a different type of technique.

### Power-Fade Tee Shot

**Conventional Method:**  Tee the ball lower than normal to promote an upright swing and position it directly opposite the left instep. Next, align your feet, knees, hips, shoulders, and the clubface to the left, essentially on the line on which you want the shot to start. Move closer to the ball than normal, so you nearly have the feeling of crowding it, and place 60 percent of your weight on the ball of your left foot, since both these keys promote an upright swing plane. Weaken your hold on the club just a little by turning both hands slightly to the left, before squeezing the handle a bit more firmly with your entire left hand, which encourages both a delayed release and a minimal degree of hand rotation.

Once nicely settled into your open setup, swing the club back slightly outside the target line, and feel as if the clubface is shut slightly—pointing more toward the ground than toward the target.

In swinging down, hold on a little longer than normal to delay the release of the hands and forearms, and concentrate on keeping your head behind the ball longer to help you hit the ball on the upswing. The delayed release, plus the insurance of the firm, weak grip, enable you to make a free and confident swing without fear of the ball going dead left. The result is a ball that shoots hard off the clubface, gets up quickly, and levels off into a penetrating trajectory as it fades gently back to its final target.

When preparing to hit a power-fade, aim your feet left of the target and point the clubface directly at the target, just like student Dennis Wang does here.

**The Anselmo Way:** *Aim the clubface at your target, and your feet, knees, hips, and shoulders left of it. Swing normally using your pitching sense, but let the hips move laterally on the downswing. The more you want to fade the ball, the more you open the clubface and the farther left you align your body.*

### Medium Iron Recovery from Heavy Rough

**Conventional Method:** Your swing objective here is to hit down on the ball as sharply as you can to keep as little heavy grass as possible from getting between club and ball and muffling the shot. To accomplish this, position the ball at the center of or slightly behind the center of your stance, with your hands ahead of the clubface at address to promote a steep backswing arc. The clubface should remain square to slightly shut. Grip the club more firmly than normal with your left hand and place 60 to 70 percent of your weight on your left foot.

Push the club straight back from the ball in an upright arc and reach your hands high. Next, pull the club straight down into the back of the ball while keeping your head steady. Because the downswing is steep, your follow-through will be restricted.

If you find it difficult to play this shot, an extra-lofted fairway metal club can come in very handy here. This is because the larger sole flattens out the grass behind the ball, so you get less resistance than you would with an iron.

**The Anselmo Way:** *Play the ball toward your right foot. Close the clubface slightly to allow for the thick grass that will open it at impact. Grip more firmly than normal. Swing the club on an upright plane, hitting down hard into the back of the ball.*

### Fairway Shot from Divot Hole

**Conventional Method:** Play the ball nearer the right foot, so the clubface is slightly hooded at the address. That way, you're in a position to hit with a very sharp descending blow. One thing to remember, however: hooding the club reduces its effective loft, so allow for this when choosing a club. For example, if the distance normally calls for a five-iron, take a six-iron, or even a seven-iron if the divot is very deep.

Keep the backswing steep and compact by pulling the club almost straight up in the air with your hands and arms.

Rotate your knees toward the target, then pull the club through with both hands in order to hit with a forceful blow and lift the ball out and up toward the green.

**The Anselmo Way:** *Take a more lofted club than normal. Play the ball back in the stance. Swing back normally. Swing down using a hit-and-hold method.*

### The Downhill Lie

**Conventional Method:** With the ball played back, stand open. Set the club-face open a hair to offset the tendency to hit a pull, and to allow for the effective loft of the club being decreased at impact.

Swing the club back on an upright plane with your hands and arms, allowing your wrists to be lively.

Swing the club down with the slope. Stay with the shot by maintaining your knee flex and chasing the ball through impact with the clubhead.

**The Anselmo Way:** *Play less club than normal. The steeper the slope, the more lofted club you should use. Play the ball toward your higher foot and use your front foot and leg as the main support post. Flex the club back and upward, then swing it down into the ball.*

### Short Pitch to Tight Pin from Light Rough

**Conventional Method:** Open your stance. The higher and softer the shot you need to hit, the more open to the target you should be. Also, open the face of

**Left:** Play the ball closer to the "higher" foot when preparing to hit a shot off a downhill lie.

**Right:** When playing a short pitch to a tight pin from light rough, position the ball forward in an open stance. This setup adjustment will promote a higher, soft-landing shot.

your sand wedge, provided there is a cushion of grass under the ball. If not, choose your sixty-degree wedge.

Play the shot almost like a bunker shot, swinging back on an upright plane with free wrist action and slapping the sole of the wedge into the grass just behind the ball. Strive for a full follow-through to encourage ample clubhead acceleration. The ball will come out high and drop softly, so you should be able to hit the ball close no matter where the pin is situated.

**The Anselmo Way:** *Play the ball forward in an open stance. Rest the sole of your sixty-degree wedge down gently behind the ball. Hinge your right wrist on the backswing, and keep the action compact. Swing down, concentrating on sliding the open clubface under the ball. If the shot is very short, use a dead-wrist method.*

When playing a shot from a buried lie in sand, it's important to hood the face of the club so you reduce its loft.

## Ball Buried in Sand

**Conventional Method:** The main thing you must accomplish is to get the leading edge of the club under the level of the ball, so that the sand pushes the ball forward and out.

In setting up, play the ball in the middle of a square to slightly open stance. Then, depending on how deeply the ball is buried, close the face of your sand wedge to a greater or lesser degree—the more buried, the more you close the face. The main reason for closing the clubface is that it gets the leading edge lower and eliminates the bounce on the rear of the flange. This way, the leading edge will dig into the sand more, as it needs to, rather than bounce off the sand and hit the top of the ball.

Make an upright swing and aim to contact the sand approximately two inches behind the ball.

You'll find that by closing the clubface the needed amount, the ball will come out of that buried lie a lot more easily than you'd think. The only problem is, it will come out much lower and with almost no backspin, so that it will run on longer after landing. If you've got some green to work with, say twenty-five feet or more, you can still hit the ball close to the hole. However, when the pin is tucked close to the bunker's lip, you should avoid trying to get too fancy; make sure you hit the green, then see what you can do about sinking a pressure putt.

One final note on playing the buried lie shot: If you happen to own a sixty-degree wedge, it can be a tremendous benefit, obviously because of the added loft but also because it features less bounce built into the flange than most sand wedges. The limited degree of bounce will allow the club to dig into the sand (and underneath the ball) more readily without the need to shut down the club and take any more loft off the clubface. The net result is that you can hit a much softer shot out of buried lies with the sixty-degree wedge. It's a great tool to have.

**The Anselmo Way:** *Play the ball nearer the right foot, with your hands ahead of it. Hood the face of your sand wedge, and hold the club over the sand about a half-inch behind the ball. Pick the club up quickly in the backswing. Hit down sharply into the sand, keeping your hands and wrists firm. Stop at impact.*

## Developing a Pro-Standard Mindset and Good Course Management Skills

Once Tiger learned the upright swing and appreciated its value, I impressed upon him the importance of the mental game, and depended greatly on the help of Dr. Jay Brunza, a United States Navy psychologist.

As soon as you or your child learns to employ a reasonably good swing technique and hit some basic shots, it's critical to learn the importance of developing mental strengths, because how good a player scores has a lot to do with what goes on between the ears. The more confident you are, the harder you concentrate, the stronger your will to win, and the better you manage the course, the better you will play.

When you think you are going to hit a good shot, you usually will, provided that your positive attitude is based on a sound swing technique that you have developed through hard practice. If you practice to groove a good swing that repeats itself, and learn a variety of shots, when you play the course you will stand over the ball very confidently and have no trouble visualizing a perfectly hit shot. As Sam Snead, Ben Hogan, Bobby Jones, Jack Nicklaus, Nick Faldo, and Tiger have proved, the stronger the shot-making image in your brain, the better chance you have of hitting a good shot when you actually swing.

The link to concentrating intensely on the course is to start thinking about your next round of golf either the night before you play or before the round. In his hotel room the night before a round, Ben Hogan used to put himself into a mental cocoon by visualizing the hole layouts of the course he was to compete on, and then play out each shot in his mind. During his most successful days on tour, when he was winning major championships, Englishman Nick Faldo used to review a few crucial shots he was going to have to play during a round—say the short-iron tee shot on hole number twelve at Augusta National during the Masters. On the practice tee, before play, Faldo would pick out the very same club he thought he was going to play on the course. Next, he visualized the perfect shot. Next, he practiced the swing he wanted to put on the ball, concentrating on making a rhythmic action.

When it came to explaining the value of the will to win to Tiger, I mentioned one man, Gary Player, and recounted one story that got the point across.

Starting on the final day of the 1978 Masters seven strokes behind leader Hubert Green, Player willed himself to victory. As Player walked down the thirteenth fairway, he pointed to a huge gallery surrounding the green and said this to playing partner Seve Ballesteros: "Seve, those people don't think I can win, but you watch, I'll show them." With a staggering display of mental maturity

Sometimes when trouble lurks, the smart move is to aim for the fat of the green, in this case left of the flag.

and fortitude, he did just that. In one of the most sensational finishes in the tournament's history, Player scored seven birdies over the last ten holes, shot sixty-four for the round, and won his third Masters. This early advice about mental fortitude that I gave to Tiger has obviously helped him. He's come from behind to win several tournaments on the PGA Tour.

In educating Tiger on the value of course management, I laid it on the line, as they say. I explained to him that even though he had a good swing and hit solid shots, he would have to learn to think even more sensibly during a round if he wanted to one day become the best player in the world. "The fact is, Tiger, you can have the best darn swing in the world, but unless you play with your head and not your heart, you will never accomplish your highest goal in golf," is what I remember saying.

Good course management comes down to two things: thinking before you act, and knowing your game and shot-making capabilities inside and out.

Playing strategically is highly critical to shooting low scores, namely because each course situation presents you with two options: playing safe or gambling. When driving, maybe you must decide whether to gamble and try to cut a dogleg, or play to the center of the fairway and leave yourself a longer second shot. On an approach, maybe you have to choose between playing for the fat of the green or attacking a hole. When putting, you must decide whether to charge the hole from twenty-five feet, and risk leaving yourself a tough comeback putt, or lag the ball up and ensure a two-putt. My point: during a round of golf you'll run into a wide variety of situations, some much more difficult than others. The state of your swing on the day, your sense of logic, your degree of confidence, your will to win, and a never-ending battle with your ego will all come into play.

Learning to proceed cautiously on the course is a chief conduit to playing strategically. Looking at the scorecard and seeing that a hole is a par four or par five should not be an automatic signal to select a driver to hit off the tee. This is especially true if the hole curves right or left, or "doglegs" as we golfers say. Often a solidly hit drive will not turn the corner of the dogleg and run into trouble. If you play a fairway wood or a long iron off the tee, you may leave

Here, the player has decided to roll the ball more softly, hitting a dying lag-putt rather than a charge-putt. You will also need to play smart on the greens if you want to shoot low scores.

yourself a longer second shot but you will be hitting from the short grass. This was Ben Hogan's philosophy, one chief reason why he won all four major championships. It's Tiger's now too, which is why he's won so many tournaments since turning pro in 1996, most notably five major championships.

Allowing for your natural shape of shot, be it a fade or draw, also plays an important role in golfing strategically and shooting the lowest possible score. If your average drive fades, then on most straight and narrow, tree-lined holes you should tee up near the right marker and aim at the trees on the left to give your shot ample room to take shape. If you usually hit a left-to-right shot, and tee off on the left side, the ball can hit the trees before it has a chance to curve back into the fairway. Only if your natural shot is a draw should you tee up on the left side of the teeing area and aim at the right center of the fairway.

If you truly want to master the course you must select a specific target on every shot. Staring intently at a section of the green up ahead satisfies your mind as to the type of shot you want to hit. Choosing the right target must be based on the lie of the ball and your playing ability on the day of the round. If the lie is clean and your swing is in form, you might want to gamble and attack the hole. If, on the other hand, doubt enters your mind, expand your target to include the wider, fat area of the green. The latter is the ideal strategy when facing a fairway wood or long iron approach, no matter how well you are playing.

Good golfers also know the average distance they hit each club, because they realize how important this knowledge is to scoring. Conversely, high-handicappers do not because they fail to take time in practice to pace off club-distances. If you know how far you hit each club in your bag, selection comes down to basic mathematics. All you do is subtract the yardage of your tee shot from the yardage of the hole, then select the club you can hit the remaining distance.

Ego also comes into play when choosing a club. Whenever you try to show machismo and stretch a club beyond its limitations, you run the risk of mishitting the ball. If you are uncertain, caught between say choosing a hard six-iron and a smooth five, always take the stronger, lower-numbered club. This strategy is best because, even if you hit the ball over the green with the stronger club, you'll be confronted with a fairly easy chip because courses are designed with very little trouble at the back of the green.

An example of a situation that calls for a stronger club is an iron off an up-hill lie. In fact, during a round I often have had to play two more clubs, owing to the steepness of the slope in the fairway.

Playing downhill shots calls for a different strategic awareness. Depending on the severity of the slope, you usually have to play one or two clubs less.

When hitting to a green well below you, hit one or two clubs less, de-pending on the degree of slope. The steeper the drop, the less club you should take. On uphill shots, reverse the strategy.

Think hard before you attempt to pull off a miracle shot from a bad lie or try to hit the ball through a narrow opening in the trees. Anytime you are in trouble, be smart enough to accept that you hit a bad shot and be willing to take your medicine. Sometimes in these troublesome situations, when you are essentially stymied, you are better off hitting the ball out sideways, back to the fairway. I know that playing safe makes you feel as if you have thrown a shot away. The fact is, if you are serious about trying to shoot a score you can be proud of at the end of the day, you must avoid compounding the error by gam-bling and hitting the ball into deeper trouble. By playing intelligently from the rough you will probably never score worse than bogey on the hole. Make a dumb mistake and you will probably have to scratch a number eight—"snow-man"—on your card or, worse yet, an X.

Another place where you have to be careful not to try too hard to make up ground is when hitting a shot from a fairway bunker. The high-handicapper who hits a tee shot down the side of the fairway, then sees the ball take a bad bounce into a fairway bunker, is not able to accept this unfortunate break. Consequently, the player tries to make up ground by playing a wood shot out of the bunker even when the lip is relatively high. What happens? More often than not the player takes a mighty swing and leaves the ball in the bunker. Don't make the same mistake. If you land in one of these hazards, play the percentages. Depending on the lie, how steep the lip is, and the length of shot, select a short or medium iron and play back to the fairway grass. The higher the lip, the more lofted club you should play.

Being overambitious will not help you save vital strokes from bunkers surrounding the green either. If the ball comes to rest near a high front lip, avoid trying to attack the flag. Play for the fat of the green, since facing a long putt is better than facing another shot from the same bunker.

You must be able to think intelligently on the greens, too. Don't fall into the trap of trying to hole out a long, breaking putt, or else you are likely to three-putt. Instead, try to lag the ball up into a two-foot circle around the hole.

As I explained to Tiger, and now to my other students, golf is a lot like a game of chess. The only difference is, you have to outthink the course instead of your opponent.

Tiger sure has come a long way, even in the last few years. Why, I remember the awful, silly, strategic errors he made at Winged Foot, venue for the 1997 PGA, and at other courses during times previous. In short, he played too aggressively, taking silly risks from bad lies.

Nowadays I'm very impressed with Tiger. Finally he's heeding the advice I gave him when he was a junior about playing stroke-play events. "Assess the strengths and weaknesses of your shot-making arsenal, then manage your game accordingly. As you improve your skills, and become more confident, begin taking more intelligent risks from the tee, and from on and off the fairway. But always play the high percentage shot and concentrate on hitting fairways and greens."

# THE
# ALL-IMPORTANT
# SETUP

**YOUR STARTING POSITION
DETERMINES HOW YOU FINISH
AT IMPACT**

I have been playing golf for almost seventy years and teaching for a long time, too. That makes me feel good. What makes me feel bad is visiting courses and witnessing golfers who ignore the fact that the address position pretty much determines the type of swing that is made. Moreover, it determines the type of contact that will be made with the ball at impact (square or off-center), and the type of shot that will be hit (on-target or off-target).

When I sit and ponder this problem, I become puzzled. That's because I know that many golfers watch The Golf Channel and listen to the on-screen teachers explaining the so-called vital elements of the setup. I also know that over one million golfers read *GOLF Magazine,* a publication that has run cover stories on the basics of the address position and the importance of it. I know too that every single teacher across this country spends at least one lesson in a series of six talking about the address. So what's the problem?

I have concluded that golfers have shut themselves off to hearing information about the setup. The reasons are, they keep hearing the same things over and over again, and they see professional golfers doing things differently than what they have read or been told by teachers.

Here, Anselmo is working with
Tiger on the setup.

If the amateur players I have talked to can serve as indicators, I know that nine out of ten golfers are familiar with the basic positions of the setup. Some follow this advice to the letter and play average golf at best. Others do their own thing because the basic tips they have received relative to the setup do not help them that much.

Golfers are right. On the whole, they have not been given anything new for the last few hundred years. In fact, if you have been playing golf for at least a couple of years, I'm sure that you too are sick and tired of hearing the same old setup tips. Don't misunderstand me. Tips such as "take a square stance," "take a neutral grip," "align your body parallel to the target line," and "point the center of the clubface directly at the target" are important points to mention. But I realized long ago that golfers need more personalized advice on the setup.

Tiger had a good setup when he came to me. But, I'll be honest, because he was inquisitive and asked me what he could do slightly differently to improve,

I started seeing that even I had fallen into the trap of thinking "If it ain't broke, don't fix it." It was Tiger who made me realize that sticking to the same old philosophies and theories governing the setup and swing can be destructive. Ergo, what I would now like to present is more sophisticated information on the setup—technical points that I promise will grab you—along with tailored tips that you can experiment with to see if they suit you better personally and allow you to play better golf.

## Grip

Many high-handicappers have been taught to use the overlap grip, simply because many professionals use this grip. Don't follow this general rule of thumb. Tiger's hands have always been small, which is why he uses an interlocking grip. Jack Nicklaus also has small hands and uses the same grip. The easiest way to learn the interlocking grip is in steps.

> **Step 1:** *With the clubhead flush to the ground, grip the club like you would a baseball bat.*
>
> **Step 2:** *Inch your lower right hand upward until its first four fingers cover the left thumb.*
>
> **Step 3:** *Pinch the sides of the handle with your thumbs.*
>
> **Step 4:** *Interlock the little finger of the right hand between the index and middle fingers of your left hand.*

Tiger and Nicklaus both prefer to use the interlocking grip because they feel it weds the hands together so there is little possibility of them pulling apart at any point in the swing, particularly at the precise moment of impact when the ball is hit. Again, many other golf pros prefer the overlap grip, employed by letting the right pinky overlap the index finger of the left hand.

The interlocking grip, shown here, is the one Tiger prefers, simply because it gives him a feeling of unity in the hands.

Whether or not you choose to use the interlocking grip is up to you, since the grip is the most personal department of the setup. However, be sure that the grip-end of the club lies across the base of your fingers and partially in the palm of your left hand, and predominantly in the fingers of your right hand. Additionally, when placing the club down on the ground square to the ball and target, the Vs formed by your thumbs and forefingers should point up at a spot midway between your chin and right shoulder. I prefer that you err on the strong side, meaning that the Vs should point toward or at the right shoulder, since this tends to give you a sense of suppleness and relaxation that better enables you to swing with controlled speed. Also, make certain that the palms of your hands face each other when gripping. When you hold the club like this, the hands will be in balance and not fight one another during the backswing or downswing. Most of the top pros—from Tiger to Fred Couples and David Duval—are going with a strong grip. But even though they turn their hands away from the target slightly, they both are parallel to each other. Try to copy this face-to-face position even if you use a very weak grip.

*TAILORING THE TIP:* As much as I worship Sam Snead and generally agree with what he says about golf technique, I wish he had never told golfers to hold the club with the same amount of pressure you would use to hold a bird in your hands. As much as I respect Jack Nicklaus, I wish he had never told golfers to try to avoid relaxing any fingers on full shots. Frankly, I argue against these two great players because I know darn well that grip pressure changes from shot to shot. Tiger, the greatest golfer today, would be the first to tell you this.

Normally, when hitting a basic driver or iron shot, you should hold the club with just enough pressure so someone who tried to pull it out of your hands would almost, but not quite, be able to do so. However, understand one thing and one thing only: When you get into hitting more creative shots, grip pressure varies. For example, when hitting a low punch-shot, you should grip more firmly to help you make a dead-wrist action. In playing a soft lob from fringe grass to a tight pin, you need to grip very lightly so you can more easily swing the club upward on the backswing, then down and under the ball going through.

In all the books I have ever read about golf, only one player ever talked intelligently about grip pressure, and that was Seve Ballesteros in the book *Natural Golf.*

Said Seve: "Advising a player to maintain just one grip pressure for all shots is as ludicrous as instructing a guitarist to always strum the chords of his instrument in exactly the same way—either fast or slowly. During a typical round of golf I make long, short, and in-between swings, in order to hit the ball crisply, softly, high or low, depending on such variables as lie, distance, and wind and ground conditions. To do all that requires frequent changes in grip pressure, all the way from very light to very firm, depending on what I'm trying to do with the ball."

## Stance

The majority of teachers recommend that students play nearly all golf shots from a square stance, meaning that an imaginary line running across the toe ends of the feet is parallel to the target line. On wedge shots they recommend that the left foot be placed a few inches farther from the target line, in an open position. In this case, a line across the feet runs left of target. I will not say this is necessarily bad advice, but I will say it is not the best advice. Although I believe that dropping the left foot back further from the target line helps promote a compact swing, I believe that players are better off standing in a way that feels natural.

The pros prove that you can be unorthodox when standing to the ball. Lee Trevino won several major championships playing all his shots from an open stance. Sam Snead played well from a closed stance (line across the feet points right of target). Greg Norman played well using a square stance for all his shots.

*TAILORING THE TIP:* If you have ever read in an instructional book or golf magazine that you should stand with your feet spread shoulder-width apart when hitting the driver, ignore this advice. As Tiger proves, and also Ben Hogan and Byron Nelson

In taking your stance, your priority should be to feel natural—not to set up according to "the book."

In setting up, go with what feels natural. Here it's obvious that this junior player feels more comfortable setting his shoulders slightly open to the target.

before him, you should stand so the distance from the outside of the left foot to the outside of the right foot is a few inches wider than the distance between your shoulders. I taught Tiger to take a wider than shoulder-width driver stance because it's been proven that this position encourages a shallower swing and an elongated flat spot through the ball, which is ideal for long driving.

## Body Alignment

This same "feel natural" advice holds true for body alignment. Most teachers recommend that the student set his knees, hips, and shoulders square to the target line. The fact is, few pros set up this way. The majority of tour professionals who like to fade the ball set up slightly open. Again, set up the way that feels natural to you.

*TAILORING THE TIP:* Some golf instruction experts, namely my coauthor John Andrisani, have noted that Tiger hits his most powerful drives when he sets his feet down in a slightly closed position and his body in a slightly open position, just like Sam Snead used to do.

According to Andrisani, this setup allows Tiger to make a power-swing more easily, without swinging full out. And I tend to agree, because as fast as Tiger swings and as far as he hits the ball, sometimes over 350 yards, he does it swinging at only 75 percent capacity relative to clubhead speed generated.

Andrisani also has observed that setting up with your shoulders open prevents the club from ever swinging too far behind the back, into what he calls the "Danger Zone." When the club swings on an exaggerated inside path, it's nearly impossible to deliver it squarely to the ball, no matter how fast you clear your hips on the downswing. The other plus-factor of the open shoulder position, according to Andrisani, is that it never allows the hip turn to be too great. When the hips over-turn, there is less resistance between the upper and lower body.

What you can conclude from reading about these nuances common to Tiger, Snead, and other top golf professionals is that not all of golf's basics are evergreen. The best approach is to test out different setup positions until you determine which one feels best and helps you produce the best shots consistently.

## Clubface Alignment

The majority of teachers say it is best to align the clubface perpendicular to the target, with the center of the clubface matching up to the back center of the ball at address. This is what I recommend, yet this advice does not apply to everyone.

*TAILORING THE TIP:* When setting up to hit a driver or another long club, some tour professionals address the ball off the toe of the club because this helps them make a slightly flatter backswing and hit with a sweeping action. Other players are unorthodox when it comes to setting up to hit medium and short irons. A surprising number of tour professionals play the ball off the heel of the club because they feel this position promotes an upright swing plane and a solid hit on the descent. Your best bet is to experiment in practice to see what clubface positions yield the best results.

Here the player is sizing up a dogleg-right hole so he can pick out a landing area in the fairway and aim the club directly at the target.

## Aim

Players who hit fat iron shots or push drives out to the right often do so because they have been taught to aim at a spot on the shot's starting line, and to stare at this spot rather than at the actual target before they swing. Don't listen to this advice, even when you see Jack Nicklaus lining up this way to hit a shot. Nicklaus lines up this way because his vision is not that good. In fact, only very rarely can he see the target. To prove this point, the last time Nicklaus won the Masters, in 1986, he didn't know that the ball he hit on the par-three sixteenth hole had landed very close to the hole.

*TAILORING THE TIP:* From my experience in talking with amateurs, I have found that those who experiment with this type of interim target aiming become disoriented over the ball and lose their imaginative powers. So unless you have bad vision and need to focus on an interim spot to help you line up square to the target, aim at the actual target. More important, look intensely at the actual target, since I believe that this focusing encourages the body to find a way to swing the club in a way that will allow you to hit the ball toward it.

## On Ball Position

Many golf instructors and tour professionals recommend playing all standard shots off the left heel. I believe in moving the ball around for different clubs. I recommend playing the driver, fairway woods, and long irons off a spot an inch behind the left heel, while the short and medium irons should be played near the midpoint of the stance. If you still think this advice is too restrictive, let me give you some other tips that will provide you with a stronger sense of freedom and enable you to take your game to the next level.

*TAILORING THE TIP:* I realize that whenever a player gets locked into one way of positioning the ball it is a recipe for trouble. The reason is, some days we wake up feeling different than on other days. If on the day of the match you wake up feeling sluggish, you should play the ball forward slightly of its normal position to give your body more time to square up the clubface. If on game-day you feel extra flexible and relaxed, you will probably tend to swing faster than normal. For this reason, try playing the ball back slightly from its normal position. Experiment in practice, before the round, to see exa*ctly* what position works best.

## Weight Distribution

The standard advice given to students by modern-day golf instructors is to place 60 percent of their weight on the right foot and 40 percent on the left foot when playing the long clubs, because this aids the shifting action of the lower body and makes the takeaway action smoother. These same teachers recommend that the player set 60 percent of their weight on the left foot and

40 percent on the right when playing the short and medium irons, claiming that it is easier to hit shots with these clubs on the descent.

*TAILORING THE TIP:* There is no set rule here, but I think that unless you are playing a specialty shot such as a low punch, you should balance your weight evenly on the center portion of each foot. Staying balanced helps you control the length of your backswing.

## Eye Position

The most common advice regarding the eyes is to look straight down at the ball on all shots. I don't agree. This position is only true for standard middle-iron shots.

*TAILORING THE TIP:* For best results on wood and long-iron shots, your eyes should be focused behind the ball. On short irons, pitches, knockdowns, and punch-shots, the focus should be positioned ahead of the ball.

Golfers who run the risk of getting visually hung up on the ball, staring at it rather than through it, hit at the ball rather than through it. Your eyes will change the plane of the swing if they focus too intensely at the ball. So be careful to realize that the ball is incidental and merely gets in the way of a good swing.

## Club Position

I am surprised that quite a high number of today's teachers recommend that their students copy Jack Nicklaus's idiosyncratic way of elevating the clubhead at address. I think a problem over the last twenty-five years has been for golf writers to talk about every element of Nicklaus's swing and setup as if they should be adopted by the masses. I have already made it clear that I don't agree with his interim-spot aiming position. Now I am going to argue against copying the way Nicklaus raises the clubhead slightly above the turf behind the ball. He claims that this setup position prevents him from snagging the club in the takeaway and promotes a smooth, one-piece takeaway of the arms, hands, wrists, and shoulders. The fact that this idiosyncratic way of setting up works for Nicklaus does not mean it will work for everyone, as Greg Norman discovered. Norman copied Nicklaus and experienced lots of tension in his arms at address, and in turn this fault caused him to pull the club away quickly just to relieve tension. He did this at the 1996 Masters, and also swung the club so far behind his body on the backswing that he found it difficult to recover on the downswing and return the club square to the ball consistently. As a result his shots lacked power and accuracy.

*TAILORING THE TIP:*   I prefer that the student rest the bottom of the club gently on the turf, like Tiger, so that its face is square to the target. This setup position promotes relaxed hands and arms, added clubhead velocity, and more controlled power.

# IN THE SWING

## A GOOD SWING IS AN UNINTERRUPTED, FLOWING ACTION

have made it very clear thus far in this book that I prefer a natural-looking swing over a robot-like motion used by many amateurs and even professionals on the lesser known tours. I'm talking about players who have taken numerous lessons during their life but failed to really make it because their swing was always being worked on. I made it very clear to Tiger before I started teaching him that I didn't want him to end up like a car that's always in the shop.

I realize that you (or your child) are anxious to improve at golf and that you are constantly lured into accepting quick-fix swing tips from friends and fellow players or from golf books and videos. You, like many other amateurs, are also probably swayed to false promises that appear on the cover of golf magazines. Typical cover lines guarantee twenty more yards off the tee, a cure for the slice in five minutes, a pro-standard putting stroke. Just the other day I happened to be visiting a golf course where I saw a back copy of *GOLF Magazine* on a table in the locker room. The cover line read, "The 5 Modern Moves." Curious, I turned to the story. A minute later the magazine was back on the tabletop. All I could do was shake my head. Every tip presented there—stronger grip, shorter arm swing, less hip rotation (backswing), more trunk rotation through impact, and the I-finish position—was old hat. Tiger has been holding the club with a strong grip since he was a child and making these other moves without even thinking about employing them. What's more, if the downswing takes only approximately one-fifth of a second from the top to impact, how in the world can you think about using more trunk rotation through impact and finishing in an "I" position rather than a "C" position? You can't.

What I found fascinating about this article was that some of the photographs are old, which confirms that the players who appear in the article, namely Jack Nicklaus and Hale Irwin, have been making these so called "modern" moves for a long time. What's more, the editors failed to mention the one move that is indeed new or "modern." Top players such as David Duval, Ernie Els, Justin Leonard, and Karrie Webb are setting the wrists much earlier on the backswing. Oh, yes, Tiger has been doing that since his junior days, but then he has always been a step ahead of all comers.

I feel sorry for golfers who are trying to improve. It seems that they are always being bombarded with new tips to try. I'm frustrated by this because I have taught one way and one way only my entire life, and my method of teaching is based on knowing what the body can and cannot do, and on what I have learned by watching the game's best players in the world at work.

I know that the PGA is working hard to standardize teaching methods. This is a good thing because when you go from course to course and work with different pros, you will know that they are not going to revamp your swing.

Trust me, the only shortcut to learning the game is to learn it right, and that simply means doing what feels natural while at the same time working within the parameters of evergreen basics.

The teachers I admire today are not really household names. I like the work of Mike Austin, a California-based teacher who during his heyday—he's ninety years old now—employed a super swinging action. Some golf aficionados said it was better than Snead's. Having played with Austin many times and seen him swing, I admit it was close. Once I got to know Mike, I understood why his swing was so good. He has a tremendous understanding of kinesiology and knows the workings of every joint in the body. Mike is still considered a rebel because he disputes the teaching theories and philosophies of many top teachers on the basis that their instruction—what they ask average students to do in the golf swing—is often beyond the student's human capabilities. This problem is compounded by the simple fact that average golfers lack the time to put in hours and hours of practice to groove a pro-like swing technique. Austin thinks many teachers ask students to do the impossible, which is one key reason golfers on the whole are still not improving. In a time when high-tech golf equipment is designed to help golfers hit the ball longer and straighter, this is pretty tragic. On the whole, teaching advancements are well behind advances in equipment design, although my coauthor John Andrisani ensures me that two other American teachers, Mike Adams and David Lee, believe, as I do, that leverage and balance play important roles in the swing.

Adams, I understand, took the time to analyze the human body and realized that players need to swing differently according to their body type, coordination, and flexibility. According to Andrisani, this Florida-based teacher streamlines the swing into three basic categories: *Leverage, Arc,* and *Width.*

The Leverage player, such as LPGA player Annika Sorenstam, is of proportional build and average flexibility. According to Adams, Leverage players use the hinging and straightening of levers (arms and wrists), the stretching and coiling of the muscles, and a tight, centered hip rotation to generate power.

Arc players, such as Tiger Woods and Davis Love, are thin-chested with long arms and maximum flexibility. The Arc player swings on an upright plane and builds power via a wide, high arc.

The Width player, such as Senior PGA Tour player Jim Albus, has a thick chest and short arms and is not very flexible. Width players rely on strong upper body rotation to generate power.

Lee, I understand, is very aware of the science of the swing and stresses the importance of balance, just as I do. According to Andrisani, this Arkansas-based instructor's highly innovative swing theory goes against the familiar "book" of fundamentals universally accepted as gospel by America's instructors. He criticizes the multitude of teachers who advise students to keep the left arm stiff in the backswing, drive the legs toward the target at the start of the downswing, and pull the club down into the ball. Even more outrageously, Lee wants instructors to start teaching students on one foot rather than two feet, arguing that this type of training encourages the golfer to make the most efficient swing possible due to a "safety envelope" around their body. Says Lee:

"It's easy to feel the safety envelope if you stand erect, with your feet touching, and without bending at the waist, then draw a circle with your body like a tree drifting in the breeze. Go as far as you can in every direction without moving the feet or bending. The circle is not very large, but there's enough latitude in it that there is no danger from falling when you stay in the center of it. Your subconscious instinct to keep your center of mass inside your safety envelope is one of the most powerful protective mechanisms in the system.

"When you learn standing on two feet, the safety envelope expands, allowing you to get away with doing all the wrong things, namely control the swing using violent upper body force. When you stand on one foot, you create a situation where any misapplied force being used to swing the club poses a threat to the body's instinct to want to remain upright. Consequently, if you train yourself by swinging on one foot, when you return to a two-foot address, you will make a more balanced, rhythmic, coordinated action that sees the body and club working in perfect harmony."

Lee's approach sounds good to me. In fact, I have many young students work on one-foot swings. Lee believes that the club is pushed back on the backswing. Like me, Lee also believes that the downswing should be a natural reaction to the backswing. Furthermore, we agree that grabbing the clubhead—increasing grip pressure and pulling the club down into the ball—is highly destructive.

## TIGER-TALK

When Tiger first visited me for a lesson, I knew that he had learned the game from his high chair by watching his father. That was a signal that he would pick up the things I wanted him to learn much more quickly if he watched me swing and looked at photographs and videos of top tour players.

Many of today's teachers and television swing analysts have their own theories on how Tiger generates such explosive power. Some think Tiger hits tee shots prodigious distances because he sets up with his feet in a slightly closed position and his shoulders slightly open. Andrisani was the first to make this observation in his book, *The Tiger Woods Way: Secrets of Tiger Woods' Power Swing Technique.*

Others believe that Tiger generates power through the strong winding action of his shoulders.

Some experts think Tiger produces power owing to the width of his arc. On the backswing Tiger pushes his hands well past his body. This, they say, helps Tiger maintain the swing radius he established at address and in the earlier stages of the takeaway. As a result he creates the widest possible arc.

Other golf teachers, such as Jim McLean, believe that Tiger generates power and torque between the upper and lower body by maximizing shoulder turn and minimizing the turning action of the hips. Tiger turns his hips only 40 degrees as compared to the shoulders, which turn 120 degrees. This ratio helps Tiger create tension or torque as he winds up on the backswing. McLean claims that this is why Tiger is able to uncoil his body so wonderfully on the downswing, snap it back toward the target so freely, and release the club powerfully into the ball.

Still other golf analysts believe that Tiger's greatest asset is the way he shifts his hips toward the target line at the start of the downswing before clearing them in a counterclockwise direction, just like Hogan. This lower body action, experts claim, helps Tiger retain his wrist hinge until the moment of impact, when he hits through the ball with lightning speed.

And then there are those who believe that Tiger's bowed left wrist position at impact, reminiscent of Hogan's, helps him hit hard.

There is no singular element of the swing that allows Tiger or any other professional to hit the ball exceptionally well with power and accuracy. This is where average golfers go wrong. They believe there is one secret, which is like believing there is one reason why London's Big Ben chimes at precise moments during the day. The swing, like the clock, is comprised of extremely complex movements. Therefore it is a combination of positions, particularly one at address, two in the backswing, and one in the downswing, that allows Tiger's swing to work so well consistently.

## SWING SECRETS: THE CHIEF REASONS TIGER HITS THE BALL SO FAR AND SO ACCURATELY

### Tiger's Number One Address Key: *Perfect Balance*

The key to good posture is standing in an athletic position. This is achieved by bending the knees slightly, leaning the torso forward from the ball-and-socket joints of the hips, and keeping the back angled but relatively straight. These elements of the address allow Tiger to balance his body weight between the ball and heel of each foot. By balancing his weight properly he allows the feet to serve as flexible balance-stabilizers. The feet support the body much like the studs of a big-city skyscraper. Tiger, like Colin Montgomerie and David Duval, arrive at the most efficient angle of incline by trying to do what Seve Ballesteros did during the 1980s when he was winning tournaments all over the world. He stands about halfway between the soldier's attention and at-ease positions. In doing thus, you want to be neither too tense nor too relaxed. You want to feel that you are standing tall, but not so tall as to eliminate a keen sense of springiness in the legs.

To finalize the ideal setup position, Tiger makes certain that his left shoulder is higher than the right, the rear end is out, and the chin is up. Be careful in copying him, that you do not exaggerate any of these positions. Tiger also takes a couple of slow breaths to help him relax. Relaxed muscles are fast muscles,

Staying athletically balanced, with the hands behind the ball, makes Tiger poised to hit the ball powerfully with the driver, fairway metal clubs, and long irons.

and thus promote high clubhead velocity. Tight muscles are slow muscles and thus cause a reduction of vital clubhead speed during the swing. If you need help relaxing at address, do what Tiger's mother Tida taught him to do: slowly close your eyes halfway, then open them. Repeat this two or three times before starting the swing.

I consider hand position to be part of the department of posture. So heed the following instructions. In setting up to play the driver, fairway metal clubs, and long irons, set the hands slightly behind the ball, like Tiger does. This behind- the-ball address will promote a low takeaway and ultimately a powerful sweep of club through ball at impact. In setting up to play the short and medium irons, position the hands only slightly ahead of the ball to promote a more U-shaped arc and more descending hit. With all clubs, avoid any upward arching of the wrists, especially the left wrist, as this will prevent the hands from working freely and fluidly.

Tiger's fairly upright shoulder-plane angle is one of his keys to a technically exceptional backswing action.

### Tiger's Two Backswing Keys: *Flexing the Right Knee and Hip, Planing the Shoulders Properly*

Tiger makes such a smooth transition from the static address to the backswing by simultaneously flexing his right knee and hip back until they nearly straighten. This right knee–right hip trigger action of the body will surprise you because it automatically causes your weight to be balanced on your right foot and leg as it should be on the backswing. By incorporating this action into your swing, you will never fall into the trap of consciously shifting your weight to your right side, which usually causes a faulty sway action.

As you swing further back and the muscles in your back start stretching more, a domino effect is created, marked namely by the planing action of the shoulders and your swinging arms which help carry the club to the top. Tiger planes his shoulders superbly, rotating them on a less upright plane than the arms and never letting them swing too far around in a clockwise direction.

**Tiger's Number One Downswing Key:** *Using a Pitching Sense to Coordinate the Speed of the Arms with the Speed of the Body*

Tiger makes a powerful windup action on the backswing, and stretches his back muscles so much that he is set to spring back toward the target. A good thought to promote a flexible backswing stretch-action is to arrive at the top of the swing with your back facing the target. All the time during the downswing, Tiger is directed by a keen pitching sense. This asset was developed in his youth and implanted into his subconscious mind long ago via the Basket Swing drill and practicing pitch shots over and over. Essentially, then, the entire downswing operates entirely on automatic pilot.

To a certain degree, yes, Tiger is consciously controlling the downswing motion. Tiger is well aware that in order to swing the hands and arms at the same speed as the body and return the clubface squarely into the ball at controlled speed, the left knee and left hip must flex correctly as the upper body tilts back. These synchronized downswing motions involving the upper and lower body are vitally important and must be practiced. The reason: if the timing and rhythm of the downswing is thrown off even a little bit, the club will finish facing left or right of the target instead of perpendicular to it at impact. The result will be an off-line shot.

Tiger's hip-clearing action is faster than any other golfer's because he has very flexible muscles. Yours will probably never be as flexible. Still, gain as much elasticity in the hips as possible by doing the stretching exercise I will prescribe shortly.

Tiger's downswing is also strong and coordinated because his goal is the *target,* not the ball. Tiger realizes better than anyone that if he sets up with good posture, triggers the backswing with a flexing action of the right knee and hip, and lets his pitching sense guide him toward the target, the club will start down correctly and find the ball.

Even though the downswing action is responsive in nature, it's better that you have a clear picture of some very important movements employed by Tiger. That way, you'll be more likely to match these same positions.

For most of the downswing, Tiger's hands stay quiet while his wrists remain hinged. Delaying the unhinging action of the wrists programs more power into the swing. Tiger knows that as long as his hips keep uncoiling, and he builds torque through resisting with the upper body, his arms and hands will drop the club down on plane until finally the wrists unhinge and the club whips into the ball.

If all this sounds complex, understand that the pitching sense you will gain from working on the Basket Swing drill will enable you to swing any club correctly. The only thing that changes is the speed of the swing. To determine your

Tiger's keen pitching sense allows him to coordinate the speed of the arms with the speed of the body on the downswing.

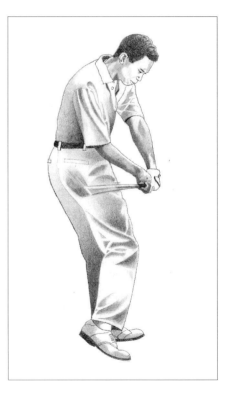

ideal swing speed, keep increasing your speed as you hit balls. Stop when shots start flying off-line, then drop back to that perfect personalized tempo.

## The Value of Exercise

Tiger could never arrive in the vital positions of the backswing and downswing with such managed care if he were not physically fit.

If you and your child want to learn to swing back fluidly, return the club-face squarely to the ball at high speed, and consistently hit stronger, straighter shots, start taking physical fitness seriously by embarking on a regular work-out regimen that includes the following stretching and strengthening exercises. In designing this daily program I concentrated on the back, legs, hips, and the hand-wrist-forearm area. That's because these parts of the body must be strong and flexible in order to create power in the swing and propel the ball toward the target more often than not.

## The Back

*Stretching Exercise:*  Stand erect with your feet spread narrowly apart and the palms of your hands flat against your lower back. Lean back as far as is comfortably possible. Hold this position for the count of ten. Return to the upright position. Repeat ten times.

This is one of the best exercises for strengthening the muscles in your stomach and lower back.

*Strengthening:* Lie flat on the ground with your legs extended. Put your hands behind your head or rest your palms gently on the floor. Next, lift your feet about twelve inches off the ground. Hold this position for one minute. Doctors have told me that this exercise is equivalent to doing one hundred sit-ups, and that it will strengthen your abdominal and lower back muscles.

## The Legs

*Stretching:* Lie flat on the floor. While keeping your left leg straight and on the ground, lift your right leg up slightly, high enough so that you can drape a beach towel under your right foot. Pull the towel gently toward you as you fully extend your leg and lift it as high off the ground as you can. Next, tug on the towel as you push your leg upward. Hold that position for twenty seconds to stretch the hamstring muscles in your legs. Rest, then repeat three times.

Jumping rope is a good way to keep your legs toned and build body stamina.

*Strengthening:*  Skipping rope for one minute or, better yet, jogging for forty-five minutes will keep the muscles in your legs toned. Additionally, these exercises enhance your sense of balance and encourage you to concentrate on tempo, timing, and rhythm—three critical links to a good swing. The legs must be strong to stabilize the winding and unwinding of the body on the back- and through-swings.

## The Hips

*Stretching:*  Stand erect, with your feet shoulder-width apart and your hands on your hips. Tilt your body to the left as far as you can go without straining. Hold the position for the count of ten. Straighten back up. Next, lean in the opposite direction. Hold the position for ten seconds. Straighten up. That's one repetition. Repeat five times.

This side-to-side leaning exercise will stretch your hip muscles.

*Strengthening:* The world's top ballet dancers work on this exercise. Stand erect with your feet relatively close together and your arms at your side. Thrust your right leg back while simultaneously lunging your left leg forward so that it forms a ninety degree angle at the knee, extending your right arm straight ahead and your left arm to the side. Hold the position for ten seconds. Repeat two times.

## The Hands, Wrists, and Forearms

*Stretching:* Squeeze a tennis ball or even crumpled-up newspaper. Hold the full squeeze position for ten seconds. Relax. Repeat a total of ten times.

*Strengthening:* Sit in a chair with your feet flat on the ground. Let the back of your forearms rest on your thighs, such that the hands and wrists are in front of your knees. Holding a five-pound dumbbell in each hand, hinge your wrists and then bring the weights toward you. Hold the position for ten seconds. Next, let the wrists stretch downward, and hold that position for ten seconds. Repeat this up and down procedure five times.

## A Healthy Diet Will Pay Great Dividends for Your Golf Game

Along with exercise, a healthy diet is important to playing good golf consistently. Tiger proves that staying away from junk food is important. Eating right teaches you discipline, allows you to feel better about yourself, which raises your confidence level, gives you stamina so you stay strong throughout the round, and keeps you trim around the stomach which makes it easier to repeat a technically sound upright swing. For these reasons, stick to a diet of whole grain cereal, skim milk, fish, chicken, beef, steamed vegetables, fruits, and pasta, and drink plenty of water. Avoid fried and fatty foods, caffeine, and soda.

# SOPHISTICATED SHOT-MAKING

## CREATIVE SHOTS YOU MUST KNOW HOW TO PLAY TO REACH YOUR LOW-SCORING POTENTIAL

**B**esides Tiger's power and short-game prowess, his creative shot-making game allows him to escape from trouble shots more easily than most of his fellow players, and this talent usually allows him to win handily.

Tiger's shot-making genius and on-course intelligence is analogous to the individual who has practical real-life experience rather than just textbook knowledge. Tiger is better able to improvise shots simply because in his early life he practiced hard with just one club and because he hit shots out of all kinds of lies. Many other players, who grew up taking lessons right from the start from a PGA pro, concentrated so hard on the mechanics involved in technique that they failed to gain feel and imagination through experimentation in practice.

Because Tiger learned to work his body and the club in different ways as a child, and made mental notes on how the ball reacted in the air and on the ground, he was better able to imagine a shot *before* swinging. Today as he stands over a shot, he plays out many different types of shots in his head, then determines which club and technique will best allow him to get the job done.

I do not want to give you the impression that common shot-making techniques taught to students by today's teachers do a disservice. In fact, I want you to read the Standard Swing Technique methods I will present shortly, since many of today's top pros play shots by following these very same directions. You may learn something that works for you.

I will also present MY WAY of teaching you to play creative tee-to-green shots—the same techniques I taught to Tiger many years ago, but that he still uses today because he believes they are simpler and easier to repeat. I believe they require you to think less and practice less, mainly because they are more natural. But you make your own decision. I don't care which method works best for you, as long as you improve and enjoy the game more—which is exactly what I told Tiger when he first visited me and I offered him the same exact choices. Let me now begin today's lesson.

### Tee Shots

**The Winding Draw:** *This is a shot used to hit a tee shot around a dogleg left, on a par-four or par-five hole that curves from right to left.*

*Standard Swing Technique:* In setting up to play this type of drive, tee up the ball extra-high so that when it sits on the tee it is well above the top of the clubface. This raised tee position promotes a flat arc of swing, which in turn allows the hands and forearms to rotate in a counterclockwise direction in the hitting area. These hand-arm actions also make the clubface rotate over at impact, which is essentially how right-to-left overspin is imparted on the ball.

To further promote a flatter swing plane, strengthen your grip by turning both of your hands a little bit to the right or away from the target. To check that you are holding the club correctly, make sure that the Vs formed by the thumbs and forefingers point to your right shoulder blade as you set the club behind the ball. The clubhead should be set flush to the ground, with the grooves on its face pointing right of target to allow for the draw shape of shot.

Even as a junior player, Tiger carefully studied the shot-situation. For example, here he is looking down at the green, already thinking out the next shot he will play.

To encourage a natural turn of the right hip on the backswing, that will open up a passageway for the club to swing on flatter path and plane, set your right foot a couple of inches farther back from the left foot—in a "closed" position.

Assume a wider stance than normal, since this will help you extend the club back low and inside the target line and create the desired powerful swing arc. Standing with your feet close together will cause you to pick up the club too quickly and thus narrow the swing arc. This fault has been proven to cause a loss in power.

To maximize the width of your backswing arc, shorter players should start moving their body laterally away from the target as soon as they trigger the takeaway. This highly unorthodox key increases the distance the clubhead travels and thereby gives you the length of swing arc of a much taller man. Taller players should simply concentrate on dragging the club back low in the initial stage of the backswing.

Going back, rotate your hips more vigorously than normal, and turn your left knee inward. When your left knee points several inches behind the ball and you feel lively tension in your right hip, you know you are wound up, ready to whack the ball.

When setting up to hit a draw off the tee, tee up on the left side of the teeing area.

When you reach the top, trigger the downswing by swiveling your knees toward the target and uncoiling your right hip so that you push your weight back over to your left side. Both of these movements help you regain your balance and truly ready you for the hit. Releasing your right side powerfully toward the target also helps you clear the left hip more quickly and easily. Once that clearing action is triggered, the arms extend out at the ball. At that point in the swing you should feel the building pulse of power being transmitted through the arms and hands. When the hands drop to a level even with the thighs, start rotating your right forearm in a counterclockwise direction. The instant this rotation begins, multiplying power starts being transferred down the clubshaft into the clubhead. Then, once you release the hands with the final, delayed uncocking of the wrists, the clubhead will be whipped into the ball while it's starting to close. This gradual closing action helps you create the desired draw-flight. This shape of shot allows the ball to follow the curve of the dogleg and land with overspin, which helps you pick up added yardage.

**MY WAY:** *Set up to the ball on the left side of the tee. Put yourself in the right frame of mind to hit a draw by visualizing a race car coming off a bank and* *veering left. At address, align your body to the right of target, on a line where you want the ball to start its flight. Close the clubface. The more draw-spin you want to impart on the ball, the more you should close the clubface and the further right you should aim your body. Swing normally.*

**The Biting Iron Shot:** *This is a shot played with a short or medium iron. It can be hit from the tee on a par-three hole or from the fairway. In several situations on short holes, for example when the hole is situated close behind a bunker on the green's bottom level, you will need to impart backspin on the ball if you want it to finish in birdie range. The object is to land the ball behind the pin and let it spin back to the hole rather than flirt with the front bunker. Backspin, or the upward roll of the ball on the clubface at impact, provides the lift force needed to keep the ball in the air and gets it to hit and dance back once it lands on the green. To impart backspin on the ball, you must strike it without making any contact with the ground behind it. If dirt or sand gets between the ball and the clubface at impact, spin is reduced, causing the ball to fly ten to twenty yards farther than normal with no bite.*

*Standard Swing Technique:* On a par-three hole, tee up the ball so that the center of the clubface, or its "sweet spot," is even with the top of the ball. Aim your feet, knees, hips, and shoulders slightly left of target to encourage a more upright out-to-in swing and a sharp descending hit. Weaken your grip by turning your hands counterclockwise a few degrees toward the target, so that the Vs formed by your thumbs and forefingers point up at your chin. Grip more firmly with both hands. On a scale of one to ten, if normal is five, you want to hold the club with a pressure of around seven.

On the backswing, make a strong coiling action of your shoulders while minimizing hip turn so you build torque between the upper and lower body and create added power. Also, swing the club back slightly outside the target line.

Here, the player has made sharp, crisp contact with the ball. The ball will carry the hazard, land behind the hole, and spin back toward it.

On the downswing, drive your legs toward the target to add thrust to the action, and pull the club down powerfully into the back of the ball.

The divot or slice of turf that flies in the air when you hit a quick-stopping iron shot has nothing to do with imparting backspin on the ball. Shaving a divot of turf on iron shots is inevitable, because of the way the club's leading edge comes sharply down into the ball.

**MY WAY:** *Play the ball close to the midpoint in the stance with your hands ahead of it. Swing the club back on an upright plane, then let the hands lead the clubhead on the downswing so you make sharp contact with the ball.*

## Fairway Shots

**The High Long Iron:** *This is an ideal shot to hit from the fairway when laying up on a par-five hole or hitting to a relatively firm green, and a wood is just too much club.*

*Standard Swing Technique:* Set up with the ball played off your left instep, tilt your left hip upward slightly, and drop your right shoulder a little more than normal, since all three of these keys encourage a powerful hit on the upswing.

On the backswing, simultaneously turn your hips and shoulders, then hinge your wrists as soon as you feel weight first shift over to the inside of your right foot. Early into the takeaway the back of your left hand should be flat and parallel to the target line—in the exact same position it should arrive at when you reach the top of the swing. Swing fully back on an upright plane and feel your weight slide into your braced right leg.

Start the downswing by moving your hips laterally. As weight transfers to your left side and your arms whip down, resist the temptation to move your head. Once the club reaches hip level you want your right hand to release under your left. The upright plane of swing you created on the backswing, together with keeping your head behind the ball, will help you achieve that goal of producing a high, soft-landing shot.

**MY WAY:** *Put yourself in the right frame of mind by visualizing a rocket launch at Florida's Kennedy Space Center. Set up normally, but play the ball further forward in your stance—directly opposite your left heel. Make an accelerated Basket Swing, concentrating on swinging through the ball toward the target.*

**The Ball-Above-Your-Feet Sweep:** *This is the shot to play on a hilly fairway when the ball is above the level of your feet. This particular sloping lie makes you automatically swing the club on a flatter arc, which produces a right-to-left flying shot.*

*Standard Swing Technique:* In setting up, make an allowance for the inevitable hook pattern of the ball by aiming your body and also the clubface to the right of the green you are hitting to. The steeper the slope, the more you should aim to the right. Choke down a couple of inches on the club, since this brings your hands closer to the ball and promotes better control. Enhance your balance by setting most your body weight toward your toes.

Make a compact three-quarter backswing, and swing extra-smoothly to help you maintain your balance.

To avoid dipping your right shoulder through impact and hitting a heavy shot as a result, maintain your body level or height on the downswing. This will promote a nice sweeping action of club-to-ball in the hitting area.

The ball will tend to draw and roll farther off this lie, so take at least one weaker club (i.e., a six-iron instead of a five-iron) depending on the severity of the sidehill slope from which you are hitting.

**MY WAY:** *At address, take a square stance, set your balance points toward the hill, choke down on the club, and open the clubface. Swing back to the three-quarter position, then through as you would when practicing the Basket Swing drill. The ball will fly fairly straight because opening the clubface compensates for the flatter swing you naturally make when hitting off this kind of slope. The*

In playing a **ball-above-your-feet** shot, balance your weight toward the hill and choke down slightly on the club.

*club will return essentially to a square impact position, so select the same club you would normally hit for the designated distance.*

**The Ball-Below-Your-Feet Hit:** *This is a shot that you will confront on a hilly course. This type of lie forces you to swing on a more upright plane and causes the ball to fade, or fly a little bit from left to right.*

*Standard Swing Technique:* In setting up, compensate for the fade-flight by aiming your feet, hips, knees, shoulders, and the clubface left of target. The steeper the slope, the more you should aim to the left.

During the swing you are likely to rock forward down the slope, so minimize this tendency by holding the club at its very end. To further preserve your balance, set more of your weight on the heels of your feet.

Swing the club back smoothly. Learn to accept the restricted length of backswing that the lie dictates. Forcing a big turn will only lead to loss of balance and ultimately a poorly struck, wild shot.

On the downswing, transfer your weight back to your left foot. Grip more tightly with your left hand to prevent your right hand from turning the club into such a closed position that you hit a violent pull or hook shot.

**MY WAY:** *Stand closer to the ball. Align your body parallel to an imaginary line that runs directly from the ball to your target, and set your balance points into the hill. Next, close the clubface more or less, depending on how severely the land falls away from you. If the angle is sharp, close it more. Next, make a normal, rhythmic three-quarter backswing, then make sure to direct the downward action with your right hand. If you swing smoothly the ball will fly almost directly at your target.*

**The Left-to-Right Crosswind Shot:** *This is a shot that you will need to play in order to conquer a swirling crosswind, common when playing courses in Florida, Texas, or in the British Isles.*

*Standard Swing Technique:* In this situation most teachers instruct students to aim their body and the clubface to the left, swing normally, and let the wind bring the ball back to the pin. The stronger the wind, the more to the left the student is told to aim. This sounds like good advice but actually it is not. The tendency is to aim too far left and hit the ball through the crosswind. Consequently, if trees, deep rough, water, or bunkers are situated left of the green, the player who follows this advice is likely to face a difficult next shot.

**MY WAY:** *I feel strongly that in this case the high percentage shot is a low-flying soft draw. To hit this right-to-left shot, set your clubface toward the target and point your feet in the direction you want the ball to go. Play the ball in the center of the stance, and further back if you want to hit a bigger draw and extra-low shot. Swing normally. The ball will fly from right to left in the air, hit the wall of wind blowing from the left, and fall softly to the green.*

**The Right-to-Left Crosswind Shot:** *This is a shot that you will need to play on a very windy day, when the wind swirls. To help you determine the general direction of the wind, look at the branches of trees and see how they are swaying.*

*Standard Swing Technique:* Many instructors believe that in this course condition it is best to aim the body and club right of target (the stronger the wind, the more to the right you should aim), swing normally, and let the ball drift back to the target. I disagree. This strategy can cause you to aim well right of target and, ultimately, hit the ball through the wind and into trouble.

**MY WAY:** *When facing a shot into a right-to-left crosswind, smart players like Tiger hit a low fade shot that starts left, hits the wall of wind, then drops to the green softly.*

*In setting up, play the ball in the center of your stance, aim the clubface at the target, and position your feet in the direction you want the ball to start its flight. Hold the club more firmly in your hands to discourage an overactive premature release of the hands and subsequent hook shot. Swing back normally. On the downswing, concentrate on trying to stop your left hand at impact so you restrict your follow-through.*

**The High Pitch:** *This is a fast-rising shot that lands softly, so it's ideal when hitting to a hard or fast-running green.*

*Standard Swing Technique:* Begin by positioning the ball forward in your stance, which ensures that you get the full value of the loft of the clubface that is essential to producing a softly hit, quick-landing shot. Spread your feet just slightly apart from the heels, with about 60 percent of your weight on your left side. Set your feet a little open, with the left foot a couple of inches farther

Anselmo demonstrates the pre-swing visualization process that's particularly important when hitting a high pitch.

from the target line. This stance limits the amount of body turn you make on the backswing and helps you clear your left side more easily as you start down to the ball, which is vital to keeping the clubface open through impact. Set your hips and shoulders fairly square to the target line at address, which encourages you to swing the club essentially on the same path you employ on full shots, which in turn promotes consistency. Finally, hold the club lightly to promote fluid hand action, with your hands in line with the clubhead and the clubface dead square to the target.

On the backswing, leave your weight left while dipping your left shoulder downward in kind of reverse pivot that automatically propels the arms and the club upward. As the club swings up in response to the dipping of the left shoulder, your upper body should actually rock a little toward the target. By the time the left shoulder has rotated under your chin and the club has reached the completion of its motion in a three-quarter swing position, your right leg is firmly braced in a straight-up-and-down position, preventing any swaying of the ball.

Trigger the downswing by gently rotating the knees toward the target, which has the effect of rocking your upper body away from it, or to your right, while at the same time pulling the club downward with your right hand. This miniature reverse pivot, or falling back movement, allows you to stay well behind the ball with your weight heavily on the right side. Also, by forcing your left shoulder upward, the action allows your left hand to pass the ball before you slide the clubface under it with your right hand.

**MY WAY:**  *Put yourself in the right frame of mind by standing behind the ball and focusing on the target. Actually see the high shot come to life in your mind's eye. Even visualize a hot-air balloon rising gently into the air if that helps you to more vividly imagine the shot. Play the ball up in the stance. Set up open for added body freedom throughout the swing. Keep the backswing compact. Coming down, let your left arm point outward in a chicken-wing position. Next, release your right hand under your left to help you slide the club under and through the ball.*

**The Pitch-and-Run:** *This is a shot that rolls a longer distance than it flies in the air. Normally it is hit from fairway grass to a fast-running green, when the hole is situated at the back of the green and there is no hazard guarding its front entranceway. This shot is normally played from as close as fifteen yards out from the green to as far as seventy-five yards. From close in, it is often played with a pitching wedge, from farther out with a seven-iron.*

*Standard Swing Technique:* Position the ball just behind the midway point in the stance. However, be cautious not to move the ball too far back, for fear of both hitting down too sharply on it and making contact before the club has time to square itself to the target at impact. Spread your feet about shoulder-width apart at the insides of the heels, and distribute your weight evenly toward the balls of both feet to promote a relatively flat swing plane.

Align your body so it's square to the target. Stand a little more upright than normal, with your knees a little straighter to further encourage a slightly flatter swing plane. For the same reason, grip the club close to the end of the shaft and set your hands only slightly ahead of the ball. Aim the clubface a little to the right of target to compensate for the touch of hook-spin you will impart on the ball due to the open-to-closed swing you will be employing.

On the backswing, rotate your knees fairly briskly in a clockwise direction, which promotes a full weight shift to your right foot and encourages your arms to swing the club on a slightly flat plane. Also, allow your head to move ever so slightly away from the target, since this discourages an early wrist break and stops you from picking the club up too abruptly. At their highest point in the backswing your hands should be at waist level. The clubface should be fanned open and your right wrist only slightly cocked.

To trigger the downswing action, rotate your knees smoothly toward the target while shifting weight back to your left foot. You should have the feeling of effortlessly pulling the clubface back to, then along, the target line, predominantly with the arms. Through impact, rotate your right hand smoothly over your left hand and your right shoulder under your stationary chin.

The shot you hit will land short of the pin, take a few bounces, then roll to the hole.

**MY WAY:** *Play the ball midway between your feet. Make a half-length backswing that is slightly flatter than normal. Let the hands lead the club into impact, then sweep through the ball. Don't go after it.*

## Off the Fairway Shots

**The Utility Wood from Rough:** *This is a smart shot to play from troublesome rough grass. Whereas the thin, light clubhead of a long iron will tend to twist and turn at impact, the heavy head of the utility wood will plow through the grass like a sickle. From as far out as 175 yards you can reach the green.*

*Standard Swing Technique:* When hitting a utility club shot from rough, you need to shorten the takeaway and narrow the arc of the swing by moving the club quickly upward on the backswing. To encourage this kind of action, stand with your feet spread a few inches narrower than normal. To further promote a short takeaway and narrow swing arc, place 70 percent of your weight on your left foot and leave it there as you make your backswing. Another important address key is to raise the clubhead above the ground slightly, behind the ball, since this prevents it from getting snagged in the grass on the backswing. Also, relax your grip on the club, since this promotes the desired high-speed whipping action of the clubhead through the hit-zone.

Swing the club on a very upright plane, rocking your shoulders more than turning them in a clockwise direction.

On the downswing, keep your head still as you rotate your right hip and leg toward the target, and swing down more rapidly than normally.

**MY WAY:** *Play the ball back, close to the midpoint of your stance, and set 70 percent of your weight on the left foot. Grip the club more firmly with your left*

In hitting a wood shot out of rough, let the wrists hinge freely and naturally on the backswing. That way you will swing the club on a more upright plane. Don't concentrate on employing a one-piece takeaway and keeping the wrists quiet.

hand to help you guide the club, and more lightly with your right to help you whip the clubhead into the ball. Swing the club up sharply, allowing the wrists to hinge freely. Swing the club down into the back of the ball.

**Medium Iron Shot from Extra-Good Lie in Rough:**  *Sometimes during a round of golf you will find your ball in rough, perched up atop the grass. The average golfer is often fooled into believing that this makes for an easy shot. That's not true. Because the ball is sitting up, the tendency is to hit up too much under the ball, causing you to add to the effective loft of the club. The typical high-handicap player, not realizing this, frequently hits the ball very high, landing it well short of the hole. Don't make the same mistake. Know how to play this shot.*

*Standard Swing Technique:*  If you normally hit a six-iron 160 yards, use a five-iron from the same distance off a perched lie. Strengthen your grip by moving both of your hands a bit to the right on the grip. This hold automatically allows you to swing the clubface from an open-to-closed position, which ultimately guarantees a sweeping action of club-to-ball through impact. Because the ball will draw slightly from right to left a few degrees, you should align yourself to the right of target when setting up. Play the ball in the middle of your stance, which is back far enough to guard against hitting up on it through impact and far enough forward to guard against hitting with a sharp descending blow.

On the backswing, pull the club back gently with your right hand and rotate your knees in a clockwise fashion to make the swing motion flow rhythmically.

On the downswing, keep your head steady as you turn your left hip counterclockwise and rotate your right side toward the target. As your hands drop down to waist height, pull the club into and through the ball.

**MY WAY:** *Play the ball more up in the stance, opposite your left heel. Take one more club than normal to compensate for hitting the ball on the upswing and hitting it higher. Raise the club slightly above the grass behind the ball to avoid getting it snagged in the takeaway. Make your normal middle-iron swing, but swing slightly slower for added control.*

**The Quick-Stopping Shot from a Fairway Bunker:** *This is a shot you will need to play when hitting out of a fairway bunker with a low lip in the 120 to 150 yard range from the green. It is the ideal shot when you have to hit the ball over another bunker or water hazard guarding the front of the green and the pin is situated close to its edge.*

*Standard Swing Technique:* To play this type of quick-stopping shot, assume a square stance and align your body to be square to the target. Fan your left foot out slightly and point your right foot perpendicular to the target line. This setup position will help you employ a powerful upright backswing and more easily clear your left side on the downswing. This hip-clearing action gives your arms and hands ample room to swing the club freely along the target line through impact.

You'll want to open the clubface a little, so to compensate for this pre-swing alteration select one club stronger than usual for the required distance. Play the ball back in your stance so you will ultimately hit it before the club starts to work its way back to the inside.

This is virtually a total hands-and-arms shot, so wriggle your feet into the sand quite deeply but not so much that you feel stuck.

On the backswing, set the club early on an upright arc and stop when it reaches the three-quarter point.

Swing the club down a little faster than normal. As you accelerate the club downward, keep your eyes riveted on a spot in the sand directly behind the ball. You'll make contact early with a slightly open clubface due to the ball being back in the stance. Consequently the ball will fade ever so slightly and land softly on the green.

**MY WAY:** *Play the ball in the middle of an open stance, and balance 70 percent of your weight on your left foot and leg. Swing. The setup position you established will promote a sharp, clean hit.*

**The Running Shot from a Fairway Bunker:** *This is a shot that you will be called on to play from a fairway bunker located farther from the green, usually on a par-five hole. The idea is to hit the ball over the lip and have it run farther down the fairway due to overspin imparted on it.*

*Standard Swing Technique:* Provided the bunker's lip is fairly low and the ball is sitting up on sand, the best shot to hit from this lie is a sweeping hook, for that maximizes the distance you'll obtain on the ground.

To play this shot, wriggle your feet into the sand only slightly. You don't want to restrict your leg action by digging your spikes deeply into the sand. Make sure that you set your right foot slightly in back of your left one in a closed position, since this encourages a flat backswing plane. Balance your weight evenly on both feet and play the ball from where you feel you can make clean, crisp contact. Be sure to set your hands in line with the ball.

Swing the club back farther inside the target line and turn your shoulders in a clockwise direction, stopping when your left shoulder rotates under your chin.

On the downswing, swing through the ball fully using a fluid release action that causes the toe of the club to lead its heel. This technique will cause the ball to turn over once it lands and run much farther than normal.

**MY WAY:** *Set your right foot back farther from the target line than your left and close the clubface slightly. Make your normal backswing, but accelerate your arms faster than normal on the downswing.*

### Around-the-Green Shots

**The Running Chip:** *This shot is played when you face a chip in the thirty to fifty foot range and there is a considerable amount of green to work with.*

*Standard Swing Technique:* Position the ball midway between your feet, setting them about six inches apart from the insides of the heels. This narrow stance brings your entire body closer to the ball so you have more control of the shot and more confidence. Also, open your stance by positioning your left foot down on the turf a couple of inches farther from the target line than your right. This position gives you a better picture of the line and provides clearance for the arms and club to swing freely through the ball. Set your shoulders square or parallel to the target line to promote a virtual straight-back, straight-through swing path. Flex your knees slightly. Set about 60 percent of your weight on your left side and keep it there throughout the stroke.

Hold the club fairly firmly, not tightly, to prevent a loose, wristy action that could cause the ball to fly too high with too much spin. Grip down a couple of inches on the club for better control. Set the clubface square to the line on which you want the ball to start rolling, and place your hands slightly ahead of the ball so that the clubshaft leans a bit toward the target.

Pull the club gently away with your right hand while keeping your wrists and lower body quiet.

Pull the club gently down with your left hand, again keeping your wrists quiet but allowing your right knee to kick in toward the target to promote a rhythmic action.

**MY WAY:** *Play the ball back in the stance. Swing back and through, keeping the hands and wrists quiet. Let the big muscles of the arms and shoulders control the stroke. A little knee action will enhance your rhythm.*

**The Extra-Lofted Floating Chip:** *This type of chip shot is played with a short iron or wedge when there is little green to work with.*

*Standard Swing Technique:* With the ball opposite your left heel, take a comfortable narrow stance and align your feet and body well left of the target. The forward ball position encourages you to stay well behind the shot at impact, which is the key to hitting a soft-landing shot. The open alignment promotes an out-to-in swing path that helps create left-to-right cut-spin. When you impart cut-spin on the ball it stops more quickly, which is ideal when you have little green to work with.

To avoid decreasing the effective loft of the club at impact and hitting a low shot, set your hands slightly behind the ball and place more weight on your right side than your left.

One key to playing the lofted chip is to take an open stance.

Swing the club back smoothly on a steep outside plane, using mostly your right hand to control the action. Then, leaving your weight heavily on your right side, swing the club down principally with your left hand while seeking the feeling of sliding the clubface cleanly under the ball.

**MY WAY:** *Play the ball just behind your left heel. Use the same open stance and balance points used for the pitch-swing. Going back, the idea is to make a lazy swing, so let the right wrist hinge freely. Coming down, the idea is to drop the club down into the ball using a ladling action of hands and wrists.*

**The Short Bunker Shot:** *This is a common shot you will be confronted with during a round. This is where the ball is approximately twenty feet from the hole and lying clean, meaning the entire ball is atop the surface of the sand. The lie is also relatively level.*

*Standard Swing Technique:* Take a stance that is open to the target about twenty-five degrees. Play the ball opposite your left heel and balance your weight evenly. Keep the head of your sand wedge above the sand about two inches behind the ball, which is where you want the club to enter the sand at impact. Open the clubface, pointing it to the right of the hole about the same amount as your stance points to the left. This sets up an outside-in swing path through the sand which, coupled with the open face, will impart a definite left-to-right sidespin on the ball. This ensures that it will sit down softly on the green when it lands.

Take the club back on a fairly narrow upright arc to about the halfway point, and allow your wrists to cock the club upward relatively early in the backswing.

Pull the club down firmly with your hands and think of slapping the sand two inches behind the ball with the bounce of the club. Bounce means the degree to which the back or rear edge of the flange lies below the leading edge of the flange when the clubshaft is held in a perfectly vertical position. The sand wedge is the only club in the bag that has this bounce feature built into the flange. The purpose of bounce is to allow the flange to glide through the sand like a knife through butter. Without this bounce the leading edge would dig into the sand behind the ball, muffling the shot and perhaps leaving the ball in the bunker.

Sand wedges are made with wider or narrower soles and greater or lesser degrees of bounce. You should select a sand wedge based on the type of sand that predominates on the course or courses you play most often. If your course has deep, soft, heavy sand, you'll find that a large-flanged club with lots of bounce will ride nicely through the sand and make your recoveries much simpler. You must be careful if the sand is shallower and lighter so that the flange hits the bunker's hard base. If the sand is thin, a large-flanged club with lots of bounce will bounce too much; it could bounce right off the base of the sand and hit the ball so it ends up flying over the green. If this is the type of sand at your home course, elect to play a sand wedge featuring a more compact clubhead that has a narrower sole and a couple of degrees less bounce.

One secret to playing the short bunker shot is making a natural-feeling, lazy swing.

**MY WAY:** *Take an open stance and aim the clubhead's leading edge at the hole. Play the ball slightly behind your left heel. Make a relaxed, syrupy type backswing, then hold the club open through impact by holding on more firmly with the left hand.*

**The Long Bunker Shot:** *This is a shot of around fifty feet, played from a bunker near the green from a good lie.*

*Standard Swing Technique:* To play this shot you must use a technique that varies slightly from the one used for the short sand shot.

Play the ball opposite the midpoint in your stance. Set up open, but avoid aiming too far left because your objective is to create a flat-bottomed arc for lower trajectory and added distance. Spreading your feet a couple of inches wider than shoulder width and setting your hands in line with the ball will promote a shallower, more U-shaped swing arc. To help visualize this shallow arc, remember what it's like to splash friends with water at the beach or in a swimming pool when they are not very close to you. In order to splash your friends, the base of your hand must contact the water on a shallow angle of descent, then skim along its surface. Apply this same principle when playing the long sand shot and you'll like the result.

The longer the shot, the less you should open the clubface and the closer the club should be to the ball when it contacts the sand. Therefore, set the clubface open slightly and focus on a spot about one inch behind the ball.

In the backswing, swing the club up to the three-quarter position, but avoid breaking your wrists too quickly. Delaying the wristcock cuts down the steepness of swing and height of the shot.

Rotating your right knee toward your left in the downswing will increase the pulling power of your hands, enabling you to drive the clubhead through the sand with the force needed to send the ball flying low and long enough.

**MY WAY:** *Take a pitching wedge. Play the ball in the middle of a shoulder-width stance. Make a Basket Swing, and concentrate on hitting a spot in the sand about a half-inch behind the ball.*

## On-the-Green Shots

**Fifteen to Twenty-Foot Downhill Putt:** *This is a tricky-looking lie because of the severe downslope between the ball and the hole. In this situation, young junior golfers and high-handicap players fear rolling the ball too far past the hole. You shouldn't.*

*Standard Swing Technique:* Most instructors suggest that students set up normally when playing a sharp downhill putt but make a softer stroke, pretending that the hole is closer to them. Anytime you have to change the speed of your stroke dramatically and start pretending, I think you run the risk of making a mistake.

**MY WAY:** *Play the ball off the toe of the putter-head, where the metal is thinner, and contact the ball with this area of the putter-face using your normal-speed stroke. This kind of impact makes for a softer hit, which compensates for the added speed of the ball due to the downhill slope.*

**Fifteen- to Twenty-Foot Uphill Putt:** *This is a tricky situation because of the severe uphill slope between the ball and the hole. Again, the severity of the slope scares junior golfers and high-handicap players because they fear leaving the ball short.*

*Standard Swing Technique:* To compensate for the uphill slope and get the ball to roll faster up it, hit the top half of the ball instead. This kind of impact will impart overspin on the ball and allow it to run up the hill.

**MY WAY:** *Imagine the hole is a few feet farther away from the ball. Focus your eyes on that imaginary hole. Next, stroke the ball more briskly than normal.*

# PLAYING
# LESSONS

## WHAT TO TEACH YOUR CHILD BEFORE A ROUND, DURING A ROUND, AND AFTER A ROUND

**B**eing the parent of a child who takes an interest in golf, because you or someone else introduced the youngster to the game, is a great responsibility. In taking on this job, you must first be very careful to let the child understand that golf is a sport, and should never be taken so seriously that schoolwork and a good education take a back seat to having fun on the course. Furthermore, if it so happens that your child progresses quickly, you must be cautious not to put so much pressure on the child to become the next Tiger Woods or Karrie Webb that their game falls apart and they no longer get any pleasure from playing the course.

In my life as a teacher I have witnessed many talented children become ruined by a parent's overwhelming involvement. By the same token I have seen other, less talented juniors grow into champions because they were coached properly by patient parents. These parents allowed the child to play and practice on their own at an early age instead of forcing them to take formal lessons soon after first picking up a club and showing an interest in golf. In Tiger's case, he showed a desire to take lessons at an early age, after appreciating how his father did such a fine job of teaching him while giving him the freedom to learn things on his own. Earl Woods, knowing that part of love is learning when to let go, decided to stop teaching Tiger himself and turned him over to Rudy Duran for further lessons. As you now know, after working with Duran, Earl brought Tiger to me, and he stayed under my wing learning the fine points of the game.

It's important for a young player to learn the basic fundamentals of setting up and swinging. But first the child must be allowed to feed off his or her own natural talent, so a teacher can have a good idea of what the student can and cannot do given the shape of their body, strength, flexibility, mental focus, and innate tendencies. Additionally, you would be surprised at how much a student can learn from practicing with just one club. Solitary one-club practice teaches the child to improvise by doing such things as opening or closing the clubface, gripping lightly or firmly, or swinging on an upright or flat plane. This type of training serves as a catalyst for turning your child into a more creative golfer.

Tiger Woods was the perfect example of someone who was *not* pushed hard by his parents. In fact, originally he was not allowed to play the course. However, once his father was certain that Tiger had utilized his inborn talent to develop a personalized technique and had been educated enough on the basics of the setup and swing, he encouraged him to play golf, where he became further educated on the art of shot-making. Sometimes Tiger golfed with his father, sometimes with Duran, sometimes with me. Tiger had such a watchful eye that he learned a lot from everyone he played golf with—about the swing, about shot-making, about the rules, about etiquette, and about the highs and lows one experiences on the course.

## TEACH YOUR CHILD THE SHORT GAME FIRST AND GIVE THEM SOME LEEWAY ON THE COURSE

Whenever I teach young junior players in, say, the five-to-eight-year-old age group, I start by teaching them how to putt, pitch, and chip. When they are ready to play the course, I give them some leeway. I feel that letting them do things such as play from the shorter forward tees greatly helps their confidence and thus prevents them from becoming discouraged. Unless they have developed exceptionally quickly, I even let them remove their ball from heavy rough and drop it on the fairway. I figure, why let them become frustrated by failing to hit the ball out of the long grass just because they are new at the game and lack the necessary strength to propel the ball out. I also let newcomers replay shots over—take a "mulligan"—if they fail on the first attempt, provided play is not slowed down. This do-over allowance helps them learn more quickly. I even will let a young junior player tee the ball up in the fairway if I feel that this will boost his or her confidence and expedite the learning process. My logic is that golf is a tough game, so by making it easier for children in the initial stages of learning, you actually lay the groundwork for developing young golfers into fine players. Expecting them to hit shots that are beyond their capabilities will simply turn them off.

## THERE IS A TIME TO LEARN TO PLAY BY THE RULES

Once a student progresses and can play quite well, then I am strict about having them play by the book. The reason is, I want the child to be able to make a true assessment of their progress. The only way to do that is to play by the rules and keep an honest score by counting every shot and every penalty stroke.

In teaching a student, I cite examples of how players have lost tournaments because they unknowingly violated the rules set down by the United States Golf Association and the Royal and Ancient Golf Club of St. Andrews. For example, player Roberto De Vicenzo lost the 1968 Masters due to disqualification after he signed an incorrect scorecard. Tommy Aaron, his playing partner, had marked down a four as De Vicenzo's score on the seventeenth hole of the final round, and a total of 66 for the round. Being so excited by his fine play, De Vicenzo quickly signed the scorecard without checking it. The Argentine superstar had actually scored a birdie three on the seventeenth hole

## PARENTAL GUIDANCE

1. Very young golfers should be supervised, on the course and at the driving range.

2. New players should learn the game backwards—starting with putting and ending with driving.

3. Junior players should establish a handicap through the local golf professional.

4. Junior enthusiasts should join their school's golf team.

5. Junior players should enter local events and those run on the national level by the American Junior Golf Association. Competition teaches players how to deal with pressure. National AJGA events expose good players to college golf coaches.

6. Watching your son or daughter take lessons can be helpful, so when they are away from their teacher you can tell them if they are making the right moves.

7. Videotaping your child's lesson can be a helpful reference, provided you can hear the pro-teacher's voice.

8. If your children take lessons from the same instructor as your neighbor's kids, encourage them all to have group discussions about swing and shot-making techniques.

9. Make sure your children know the rules that apply to the most common course situations, such as lost ball.

10. Teach your child the basics of good course etiquette.

Playing by the rules, set down in a book by the United States Golf Association (USGA) is very important.

and shot a final round of 65. Still, because the total score was attested by virtue of De Vicenzo's signature, he was disqualified.

Another example of a player being hurt by not knowing the rules, and one I share with students, involved 1982 Masters champion Craig Stadler. The incident took place during the third round of the 1987 San Diego Open, when Stadler was in contention to win the event and take home some big money. On the fourteenth hole the only way Stadler could tackle his shot from under a tree was to kneel down and hit it. He did just that, but unfortunately he violated the rules by kneeling down on a towel so as not to dirty his trousers. The moral of the story is stated by Stadler himself in the book *I Am the Walrus,* which he wrote with my coauthor John Andrisani:

"Become more familiar with the rules. And, whenever you're in some type of course situation where you're not completely sure of a particular rule, ask your playing partner about your options."

As Stadler makes evident, the trite expression "If it feels good, do it" certainly does not apply to the rules of golf. I accept the fact that a player is able to get free relief from such circumstances as casual water, ground under repair, or finding his ball in a hole made from a burrowing animal. However, most of the time, if you break the rules you can be expected to lose the hole in a match-play competition and be penalized two shots in a stroke-play competition. When all is said and done, nevertheless the rules are there to help you.

You must know the rules before they can help you save vital strokes. If you don't, I promise that you will pay a dear price in a formal stroke play competition or match play tournament. Learning the rules takes some effort, but your study-time will be worthwhile. Being well versed on the rules saves you the embarrassment of breaking them out of ignorance, saves you vital strokes by allowing you to drop the ball from severe situations, and can prevent you from losing a hole or being disqualified.

Ideally you should learn all the rules contained in the book *The Rules of Golf,* so that you can teach your child. Failing that, teach them the most common rules and procedures of etiquette that follow, so that they do not hinder the play of other golfers.

## THE BASIC RULES: *DO'S AND DON'TS*

### Out of Bounds

*Situation:*  Your child hits a drive that slices well right of the fairway and into an area past the white out of bounds stakes bordering the course.

*What Not to Do:*  Do not allow your child to drop a ball next to the spot where the ball entered the out of bounds area under a penalty of one stroke. This is a common error made by parents and junior players.

*What to Do:*  Instruct your child to re-tee the ball from the teeing area, where the last shot was played, under penalty of one stroke. In other words, the child must play the third shot from the tee.

### Bending or Breaking Branches

*Situation:* Your child's approach shot to the green lands near a tree, with branches overhanging the lie.

*What Not to Do:* Do not allow your child to bend or break branches to make it easier to take their address or swing. This action is a clear rules breach.

*What to Do:* Advise your child to physically take a stance, and if you can see that he or she is about to violate the rules, instruct them to declare the ball unplayable.

### Grounding Club in Hazard

*Situation:* Your child hits a shot into a bunker guarding the green.

*What Not to Do:* Do not allow your child to rest the club on the sand when addressing the ball to hit a shot out of a bunker. That false move constitutes a rules breach.

*What to Do:* Advise the child to raise the clubhead off the ground when playing this type of shot, usually above an area of sand two inches behind the ball, and keep it elevated off the sand during the initial stage of the backswing.

### Lost Ball

*Situation:* Your child hits a shot into the light rough but cannot find the ball within the designated time of five minutes allowed by the rules governing the game of golf.

*What Not to Do:*  Don't let the child think that golfers are allowed to drop the ball near where it was lost and simply take a one-stroke penalty.

*What to Do:*  Instruct your child to incur a one-stroke penalty, then return to the place where the last shot was played and hit a new ball from there.

## Lateral Water Hazard

*Situation:*  Your child hit a drive 150 yards in the air and it landed in a lateral water hazard marked by red stakes. The ball last crossed the margin of the hazard seventy-five yards off the tee.

*What Not to Do:*  Do not allow your child to take a one-shot penalty and drop in an area of fairway even with the spot where the ball splashed down into the water.

*What to Do:*  Advise your child that according to the rules there are some correct options available under a penalty of one stroke, including 1. Dropping the ball two club-lengths from the point where it last crossed the hazard, and playing the ball from there and, 2. Keeping the point where the ball last crossed the margin of the hazard between themselves and the hole, then going back as far as they wish to play the shot.

## Removing Loose Impediments

*Situation:*  Your child hits a ball onto a grassy bank within the bounds of a yellow water hazard. But a small stone is right where your child's right foot will need to be placed for the next shot. The child is about to move that stone, not because it presents a danger but because it hinders the stance.

*What Not to Do:* Do not allow your child to lift the stone and toss it out of the way. Players are not allowed to touch or move loose impediments that lie within the boundaries of a hazard.

*What to Do:* To avoid being penalized, your child should make a minor stance adjustment in order to employ a swing.

## Touching Line of Putt

*Situation:* Your child's ball is on the green. While getting ready to putt, the child notices a spike mark in the line of the putt. The child wants to tap down the spike mark with the bottom of the putterhead.

*What Not to Do:* Don't let the child touch the spike mark, since this qualifies as a rules violation.

*What to Do:* Advise the child that players are only allowed to fix ball marks on the putting line. Further, instruct the child to hit the putt a little more firmly so the ball will be less affected by the spike mark, and let luck take its course.

## Carrying Too Many Clubs

*Situation:* Your child wants to carry an extra driver, making the total number of clubs in the bag fifteen.

*What Not to Do:* Do not let the child play with more than fourteen clubs, since that is the maximum number permitted according to the rules.

*What to Do:* Advise the child to consider leaving another club behind instead, maybe a long iron for example. That way the extra driver can still be carried and your child can experiment with it on the course without being penalized.

## Waiving the Rules

*Situation:* In a stroke play competition, your child's playing partner discovers on the eighteenth tee that he has been playing with fifteen clubs, one more than allowed by the rules. Because your son knows that his playing partner did not use that club during the round, he is considering not saying anything about the rules breach.

*What Not to Do:* Instruct your child not to let the player get away with the breach. If your child agrees to waive the rules, both players are disqualified.

*What to Do:* Instruct your son to call a member of the tournament committee or to immediately make his playing partner aware of the rules breach. In this case, your child's playing partner would be penalized the maximum of four strokes.

## The Basic Rules of Golf Etiquette

In going around the course with your child and two other players, make sure that the young golfer:

1. Arrives at the course looking neat and wears golf shoes—not sneakers.

2. Never stands directly in a fellow player's line.

Do not stand in the line of a fellow player while he is putting.

Do not disturb a fellow player by conversing loudly with others.

3. Avoids talking, jingling change, rattling clubs, or opening the Velcro strap of their golf glove while a fellow player swings or prepares for a swing or stroke.

4. Avoids taking too much time to play a shot or to move on after playing a shot.

5. Does not walk too far out ahead of a fellow player who is preparing to play a shot.

6. Is careful not to step in another player's line when walking on the green.

7. Does not drive a golf cart on the front entranceway to a green, through the fringe, or over a green.

8. Replaces a divot in the fairway after hitting a shot.

Rake the sand after playing a bunker shot.

Do not step in a fellow player's line on the putting green.

9. Repairs his or her ball mark on the green.

10. Rakes the sand in a bunker after a shot is played.

11. Shows good sportsmanship.

12. Does not hit into slower players.

## The Art of Teaching a Junior

If anybody disputes the fact that teaching is an art, tell that individual to come and debate this subject with me. Make no mistake, it is especially an art when your own child is the student.

Even if your child takes lessons regularly from a local golf professional, you have a huge responsibility every single time you play golf with your son or daughter. You must remain patient, you must know what to say and what not to say about swing technique, you must be honest yet not harsh, you must be encouraging, and most of all you must be your child's friend. Your goals should be to find ways to help your child play a better game and to have fun in the process. Let's look at how you can help your child improve their game before and during a round, then get into the fun games you can play.

Before the round make sure that your child loosens up and stretches to guard against injury, and to give them the best possible chance of making a fluid swing. You can purchase a weighted training club for your child to loosen up with, or make one yourself. Many pro shops and discount outlets offer this specialty item or weighted circular donuts that can be snapped onto the shaft of the club near its neck.

To make your own weighted junior club for your child, just cut down an old driver that you won't be using. First, remove the grip. Second, use a pipe cutter to trim the shaft down to the length required by your son or daughter. Third, pour a substantial amount of sand or lead pellets down the shaft. Fourth, put a new grip on the club. If you haven't worked on clubs and are not sure of your workshop talents, you can always have this done at your local golf pro's repair shop.

The key things to tell your child are to practice swinging the weighted club very slowly and fully, and to concentrate on employing a fluid movement, not a fast movement. Remember, the child is wielding a heavier club, so to avoid injury it should not be swung at anything like normal speed. Swinging the training club will cause the muscles in the back to stretch, so when the child reverts back to a regular driver, their windup action and power quotient will increase.

Once the loosening-up is completed, check your child's address. Place one club across the toe-ends of your child's feet, and another stretching straight back on-target from a point about three inches behind the ball. Next, stand behind the child. If your child is standing to the ball correctly, the toe-end club will be parallel to the second club that represents the target line. If the clubface is aiming well left of the target, there is a good chance your child's

Checking your child's grip is important when you consider that the grip is commonly called the "engine room" of the setup.

hands are set well behind the ball, and the ball is too far forward in the stance. Setting the clubface down so it aims well right of target is usually caused by the reverse of these two faults, setting the hands too far in front of the ball, and playing the ball too far back in the stance.

Another aspect of your child's address position that should be checked is the grip. You want to make certain that the palms of the hands are parallel to one another. It doesn't matter whether the youngster uses an interlocking or overlap grip, or a strong or weak grip, both hands must be parallel to each other if they are to work as a team. As Jack Nicklaus has said repeatedly, "Golf is a two-sided game."

Making sure that your child has good posture is also critical to good performance. Stooping over is common among junior players learning the game. This position feels more comfortable but it is not correct. It causes a quick pick-up action of the club on the backswing and an overly steep downswing. The result: skied drives and fat iron shots. It's your responsibility to stress to your child that standing correctly, according to the address tenets I laid out in chapter 3, is a vital conduit to swinging the club on the proper plane and hitting powerfully accurate shots.

While you are checking your child's posture, be sure that the chin is not resting on the chest. In order for the natural turning action of the shoulders to be preserved, the chin must be up slightly, a few inches from the chest. Show your child what's right.

Once you're satisfied with your son or daughter's setup, check the swing. Make sure that the child does not overuse the hands and pull the club well inside the target line on the backswing. Remind the junior player of the importance of letting the big muscles control the swing rather than the small muscles. Also, let the child know that more success comes from swinging the club on an upright plane than on a flat plane. Finally, let them make a few basket swings.

If your child's swing is so fast that it throws them off balance, mention that distance is not only a result of clubhead speed but of hitting the center of the ball with the center of the clubface. And when you swing too fast and lose your balance, you cannot accomplish this goal. To help your child slow down, suggest hitting the driver only as far as a normal seven-iron. After hitting about ten balls while thinking of this tip, the child will iron out any tempo problems and be ready to swing the driver at an easy-to-control pace.

In checking your child's swing, avoid getting overly technical. However, look carefully at the full swing in certain key positions: in the takeaway, halfway back, during the initial upward move, at the top of the swing, during the first move down, at impact, in the follow-through, and in the finish. Obviously the swing is mechanically complex and fast moving, so it would be better to record the elements of the swing with a video camera. That way you can give your child instant visual feedback. I now want to cite specific checkpoints for you to observe, either with your eyes or through the lens of a camera.

## The Takeaway

Make sure that the child triggers the swing by flexing the right knee back slightly. Once the child's swing is in motion, make sure that their left arm stays

In the initial stage of the takeaway, the club should swing low to the ground.

extended in a relaxed, tension-free fashion and guides the club back low to the ground for about six inches while remaining dead square to the target. The left knee should move outward slightly, then inward. The right hip should be moderately coiled with your child feeling a stretching sensation. You never want the child to twist the right hip, otherwise the club will swing too far inside the target line. Let your child know that the right hip is a valuable swing trigger. The smooth coiling rather than violent twisting of the hip encourages the right leg to brace sufficiently to hold the body's weight.

## Halfway Back

The shaft of the club should be parallel to the target line when it reaches a point level with your child's waist. The wrists are firm and the muscles in the

As the club swings upward, the left wrist should be flat— not cupped as some modern teachers believe is correct. The right wrist should hinge freely and naturally.

back are used to control the swinging action of the club. Make sure that the child feels a connection between the movement of the arms and shoulders, and the movement of the club. The hands should be pushed past the body, with good extension to create a wide arc, while staying in front of the body— just like in the Basket Swing drill.

## The Initial Move Up

The swinging weight of the clubhead should cause your child's wrists to hinge automatically, the right more than the left. Make sure your child clearly understands that the hinging action of the wrists is not a conscious move. Make sure too that the child understands that the right leg should be braced. Bracing the right leg serves essentially as a wall for your child to wind around as the swing back continues, and this is critical to controlling the club and maximizing torque that ultimately translates into power. The toe of the club should point at the sky when the hands swing past the waist. The left wrist should be flat.

### At the Top

The child's weight should be balanced mostly on the right foot and leg since that is the pivot post for the backswing. As the child coils into his right side, he will feel that the left heel wants to be pulled off the ground. It's okay that the left heel be allowed to lift. Tiger has always been flexible enough to make a strong windup without needing the added freedom of a rising left heel. Your child, or you yourself, might do better to let the left heel lift up if that alleviates a feeling of restriction. The child's back should face the target and you should see wrinkles in their shirt or blouse. Ideally the clubface should be square, or midway between the horizontal and vertical positions, at a forty-five degree angle. The back of the left hand and wrist should remain flat and line up with the outer area of the left forearm.

### The Initial Move Downward

Some teachers believe that turning the left shoulder or left hip counterclockwise should be the trigger for the downswing. Others believe that the player should start the downswing by replanting the left heel. I don't believe that either of these keys is natural. I explained to Tiger that if you are right-handed, it is much more natural for the right side to control the downswing. After all, when holding a basketball in both hands and wanting to toss it forward after winding up, it is your right side that releases the power.

Since the downswing takes only one-fifth of a second, once it is triggered the child has no time to think about making specific swing movements involv-

The accompanying photograph clearly shows how the left hip flexes back on the downswing.

ing the body and club. In fact, by consciously trying to move the club, the flowing continuity of the action will be disrupted and a poorly struck, off-line shot will result. If your child appears to swing at the ball rather than through it, there is too much going on in the head. Impress upon your child to just let the downswing happen. To help promote a natural action, have a "problem child" practice the Basket Swing drill.

A child who swings down correctly will sense a feeling of effortlessness as the arms, hands, and club fall freely, the left hip flexes back, and the body catapults toward the target. This feeling of effortlessness means that the timing and rhythm of the swing are very good.

Even though the downswing operates essentially on automatic pilot, you must make sure that your child is in certain positions in order to return the club squarely and solidly into the ball at impact and swing freely through. For example, your child's left hip should have flexed considerably to the left of target

in a counterclockwise direction, while the left knee and leg stabilized themselves and became a solid, balanced pivot-post. The left leg does not drive
toward the target as most golfers believe. The left leg and foot control the balance and equilibrium of the downswing.

## Impact

Most of your child's body weight should be balanced on the left side, with the
left hip and knee flexed back. At the precise moment of impact the left shoulder, the back of the left hand, and the clubhead should all line up. Also, the
palm of the right hand should be square to the target as well as the shoulders.
However, the left shoulder should be raised up; it has to be in this position for
the child to make a solid upswing through the ball.

## Follow-Through

The follow-through is a direct reflection of prior movements and ideally should
be attained automatically. Having said this, it is highly important for you and
your child to know that when the club reaches waist level in the follow-through,
its shaft should be parallel to the ground with the toe pointing upward. The
back of the right hand and the right arm should be parallel to the target line.
The right shoulder should be brushing an area under the chin and the right
arm should be extended. The right arm and for that matter the entire right side
provide the extension in the swing. All objects pitched, tossed, or thrown are
released through the right side while the body is balanced by the left side. To
a large degree this release is instinctive and directed to the muscles by the
mind's reflex action.

Having children visualize the ideal positions involved in the follow-through
better allows them to employ a free-flowing motion essential to accelerating

the clubhead through the ball at maximum controlled speed. This is the advice I gave Tiger when he first started taking lessons from me, and it's obvious from his fine play that he never forgot my words of wisdom.

## Finish

Here, your child's stomach should face the target. The body should be erect, with as much as 95 percent of weight balanced under the left foot and the remainder on the toe of the right foot, the only part of it touching the ground. Both arms should be comfortably bent at the elbows as the hands come to a stop at a point level with or slightly above the head. These positions, in their entirety, confirm that your child has swung the club freely and powerfully, yet with maximum control of the body and club.

A balanced finish indicates that the movements of the swing were rhythmic and technically correct.

Examine your child's pitching setup, since to a large degree it determines how he will swing.

## Short-Game Checks

Only swing checks have been discussed thus far. It is also important to take the time to watch your child hit pitch shots, chips, sand shots, and putts before the round, and point out any noticeable technical flaws.

*Pitching Setup and Swing Checks:* Make sure that your child sets the hands ahead of the ball, balances weight on the left foot, chokes down slightly on the club's handle, controls the club's direction with the back of the left hand, and swings through the ball. You do not want to trap the ball when playing the standard pitch.

*Chipping Setup and Swing Checks:* When hitting a normal chip, check that your son or daughter plays the ball near the midpoint of a narrow stance, hinges the right wrist on the backswing, and swings down quite steeply so the

On chip shots, make sure that your child lets the right wrist hinge slightly on the backswing.

ball is struck on the descent. It's also critical that the left wrist stay firm through impact.

*Bunker Play Setup and Swing Checks:* When playing a normal bunker shot, check that your child sets up open, aims the clubface at the target, and swings through along their body line.

*Putting Setup and Swing Checks:* Make certain that your child keeps the head and body still while controlling the stroke with the arms. On longer putts and on slow greens, a slight degree of wrist action is permitted.

## The Right Golf Attitudes

If you already play golf, you know only too well that it can sure wear you down mentally, particularly if you are not prepared for the inevitable low points during

Be sure the child swings through on bunker shots and does not try to scoop the ball out of the sand.

a round. When I first started playing golf with Tiger, I constantly reminded him to have the courage to hang tough and stay positive when things weren't going his way on a very difficult course. I also told him not to let whatever problems he had up to the present moment have any influence on the shots he still had to play for the remainder of the round. The secret to scoring well is to keep visualizing the perfect shot before you swing and to do whatever it takes to stay tension-free, such as breathing in and out slowly or thinking for a second about a sandy beach. Your child must be told that self-discipline and the ability to stay focused no matter what happens is a link to becoming a more complete player. The child who holds his course in the face of adversity and weathers the on-course storms will be amazed at how quickly things can take a turn for the better.

A confident attitude, like courage, is also a prerequisite to playing good golf. Once a child develops the correct setup and swing fundamentals, it's essential that they stick with them and have faith in them. The principles I'm

Many golfers don't realize that the sweet spot of the putter-face is closer to the heel of the club. Be certain that your child considers this when lining up the putter-face to the ball.

describing will work for any junior golfer within the limitations of the player's athletic ability. The child must have faith in their game, especially if their action is a little unorthodox. Don't let your child let a faulty swing or even a few high scores throw them off track and start them down the futile road of searching for Band-Aid cures. Instruct the child to have faith in their technique, and work through any problems that occur during play.

In preparing your child to be a more complete golfer, offer a reminder on each shot to concentrate intently on the fundamental movements of the setup and swing, taught already to them by me. If the child follows these instructions it is highly unlikely that an occasional bad shot, a needling opponent, or a bad bounce will become distractions.

To become a winner, your child must also learn to be "dumb like a fox" on the course, just like Tiger is. When the game is on, Tiger lets other players worry like crazy about lurking hazards while he focuses so keenly on his target, he never notices the trouble and hits the ball close to the hole. Teaching children this same attitude will help them evolve into junior champions much more quickly.

## Games People Play

Let's address the fun aspect first. I think you will make golf more amusing for your child if you play games during a round. If you play a decent game and your child is very new at golf, you can probably afford to give the youngster two strokes on par-three holes and three strokes on par-four and par-five holes. During a match, where the player with the lowest score wins the hole, you play from the back tee on every hole while your child plays from the front tee. Additionally, divide the match into three parts, with one point going to the winner of the front nine, one point to the winner of the back nine, and one point to the winner of the overall match. This is the standard Nassau format. If you wish, to stir in more competition and possibly have more fun, play six three-hole matches. Whatever it takes to make the match competitive, and whatever wager you use as a competitive incentive, the object is to make the game fun. For example, if you lose, you wash the car and dump the garbage. Or, maybe you could double your child's allowance for the week. If the child loses, they clean out the garage and wash the car.

The higher the standards of your family's junior golfer or golfers, the more competitive you can be with them, the higher the goals you can help them set for themselves. Sadly, I have seen fathers get a kick out of beating their kid, in the hope that this will make their child even more determined to win the next time. Never mock a child when they lose. This, as I suspect you feel, will hurt them greatly.

It's okay if you sense that your child is not up to competing with you. Instead, challenge him in other ways. For example, tell your child to try to hit the ball out of the bunker on the first shot every time during the round. Challenge the child to have no three-putt holes during a round. Children who are really improving fast can be challenged to make three par scores in a row or two birdies over eighteen holes. The bottom line is, be creative and devise ways for the child to stay focused on the game while having fun.

## On-Course Lessons

While playing a round of golf with your child it's also essential that you keep them interested in the priority of scoring and offer a tip here and there. Let's go over some that are simple and that can help immensely.

*Tip One:* To ensure that your child aims directly at the target and swings through the ball toward it, tell him to imagine a tunnel. This imaginary tunnel should stretch from the ball to the target. Alternatively, tell the child to imagine a ring-of-fire or a big round circle to hit the ball through. Using images stimulates the child's brain and takes their mind off the pressure of scoring. So be creative, even wild. If the child hits accurate shots via the use of imagery, good scores will result.

*Tip Two:* To hit a quick-stopping cut-pitch shot, instruct your child to play the ball midway in the stance and aim the clubface and the body slightly left of target. Also, have the child put about 60 percent of their body weight on the left foot. This last setup adjustment will promote a short takeaway and steeper swing.

On the backswing, the club should be swung slightly outside the target line.

On the downswing, the club should be swung slightly across the ball.

The shot your child will hit as a result of following the aforesaid directions will fly slightly from left to right. The ball will also fly high and sit down softly the moment it hits the surface of the putting green.

*Tip Three:* To hit a chip off hardpan, have your child use a pitching wedge for short shots around the green and a seven- or eight-iron for longer chips.

One important key to playing a short chip off hardpan is to position the hands well ahead of the ball.

Also, tell the child to toe the club in slightly to compensate for the clubface opening a bit at impact.

Additionally, to ensure clean, crisp contact at impact, instruct the child to set their hands ahead of the ball at address and keep them leading on the downswing.

*Tip Four:*  To help young golfers read tricky breaks in greens, give them the following instructions for plumb-bobbing the line:

Stand with your body perpendicular to the horizon and hold the putter at arm's length in front of you, with only your thumb and forefinger securing the top of the grip. Let gravity ensure that the putter hangs vertically. Next, obscure the ball with the lower part of the clubshaft, then close your nondominant eye. If the shaft now falls to the right of the hole, the putt will break from right of the hole to left of it. If, on the other hand, the shaft appears to the left of the hole, the putt will break from left to right.

*Tip Five:*  When your child faces a putt in strong wind conditions, have them widen the stance to promote good balance, bend more at the knees to enhance leverage, and employ a shorter stroke for added control.

## Post-Round Analysis

The job of being a responsible golfing parent does not come to a halt once you complete a game of golf with your child. I realize this may not sit too well with parents who have a busy schedule, but try to understand the benefits that golf can bring to your son or daughter at a young age and forever. Learning golf teaches your child trust, honor, friendship, determination, discipline, and patience. Of course, it goes without saying that golf also teaches children the "good life" and helps keep them off the streets. Further, children who develop into even decent players stand a better chance of taking giant steps in the world of business since the course is the ideal place to "network." And, young golfers who develop a high-standard game can earn millions of dollars playing golf professionally.

Because of the benefits that golf can bring, don't let the child's round stop after they complete the eighteenth hole. Take your child to the nineteenth hole for a soda and spend some time analyzing the good and bad golf shots in the round.

After a refreshing drink and a brief analysis session, visit the practice tee. Just like they say a married couple should never go to sleep until they have ironed out a problem in the relationship, you should not leave the course until you have helped your child trace a fault in the swing and iron it out on the practice tee.

## My One Lecture to Juniors

One of the things I give myself the most credit for is helping develop the game of golf's present-day best player in the world—Tiger Woods. However, I now have a new stock of up-and-coming players who are long off the tee, super-accurate with their iron shots, possess an excellent pitching, chipping, sand play game, and can putt the eyes out of the hole. What makes me the happiest is not how well my students play, but how hard and diligently they all work to develop their skills. In fact, as good as any one of my students is, each continues to work hard in practice. Just like Tiger, they believe there is such a thing as the perfect swing, thus there is always room for improvement.

You must be disciplined enough to practice after a round, to fix a faulty swing or improve a good one, even if that means not sitting on the beach with friends and taking in the summer sun. Fortunately, Tiger loved to practice, and I know he still does. That's because I gave him a formula for improving all areas of his game, from the setup, to the swing, to fairway shot-making, to trouble play, to the short game, to putting.

So far I have given you and your parents a game plan for improvement, including tips on how to prepare on the practice tee before a round and how to make working on your game fun during a round. Now, I want to address how you can improve at golf after the round and in your spare time.

Even though one of the hardest things to do is report to the practice range following a bad round, most top Tour pros do it, including Tiger. That's because fine players believe it is best to try to trace a fault in the swing and fix it, in the same way race car mechanics look for a problem in the engine of a car and repair it as soon as possible. Unless you are truly mentally and physically exhausted, it's important for you to pinpoint what went wrong with your game during a round, then correct it during your post-round practice session. If you do not, you will run the risk of forgetting your problem, and the problem will get worse.

If you lack the time to visit the practice tee after a round for a hard session, at least take time to jot down your obvious swing faults so you remember what to work on.

If you lack the time to work out the problems you experienced on the course, such as hitting a slice off the tee on most holes, hitting approach shots fat, failing to loft the ball out of bunkers, or pushing putts, make time to jot down your shot-making faults. That way, when you feel fresh physically and mentally, you can refer to your notes and work on correcting your faults.

If you feel ready to iron out your faults after the round, I suggest you start by checking your setup. Stand in front of a mirror or pane-glass window, look at your address position on video, or have a friend check the position of your feet, knees, hips, and shoulders. It's usually a small thing that causes big problems in your swing and shot-making game. For example, often a hook problem off the tee can be traced to a very strong or light grip.

One glaring difference between top pros and the majority of junior players is that pros know their bad tendencies, and thus it is easier for them to single out what's causing their shots to fly off-target. If they can't figure out a solution, they can rely on their professional coach to help them swiftly put their swing back in good order.

I worry about you juniors who do not take lessons from a golf professional or even a parent who is a fairly good player and very knowledgeable about golf technique. This is my worry: I do not want you to look for quick tips or listen to strangers you meet on the driving range. If you do listen to every Tom, Dick, and Harry, you will become so confused that just starting the club back will be a problem, let alone returning it squarely to the ball and hitting a good shot.

So that you don't fall into the trap of becoming gullible and letting your natural talents go to waste, what follows are descriptions of the most common bad shots, along with possible causes and remedies. I want you to work hard to know what triggers a bad shot, since this is an important part of evolving into a complete golfer. You must work hard to know your game, so when things don't go exactly as planned during a round you can fix a swing problem quite quickly and put yourself back in the match.

**Fighting a Common Tee-Shot Problem**—*The Push Slice* (A shot that veers off to the right of target more abruptly than a fade).

A simple adjustment in ball position can cure your push-slice problem and help you wallop the ball down the line in the tightest quarters.

**Causes:** Setting up open, playing the ball too far forward in the stance (i.e., off the left instep), swinging out at the ball, and concentrating on driving the legs toward the target can all cause you to arrive at impact with the clubface open and hit a push-slice shot.

**Cures:** Position the ball opposite your left heel or an inch or two farther back in the stance, practice the Basket Swing drill to help you relearn the proper natural movement of the legs, and concentrate on letting the club swing down the line and up through the ball. One or more of these tips will help you return the clubface squarely to the ball at impact and hit powerfully accurate shots.

**Fighting a Common Approach-Shot Problem**—*The Fat Medium Iron* (A heavy shot that falls well short of the target).

**Causes:** Placing 70 to 80 percent of your weight on your left side at address, playing the ball behind the midpoint of the stance, setting your hands a few inches ahead of the ball, reverse-pivoting and swinging the club back on an overly steep plane, pulling the club down too fast with the hands, and concentrating on swinging at the ball instead of through to the target can cause you to hit a fat iron shot.

**Cures:** To prevent this weak shot, balance your weight evenly or place only slightly more weight on your left foot. Also, play the ball near the midpoint in the stance, set the hands in line with the ball or just slightly ahead, let your back-stretch action help you swing the club away on the proper plane, and allow your Basket Swing throwing instincts to control the movements of the body and club on the downswing.

**Fighting a Common Short-Game Problem**—*The Thin Chip* (A shot that flies extra-low and either runs well past the hole or through the green).

A slightly open stance will encourage a free rather than tense chipping swing and allow you to make pure contact with the ball.

**Causes:** Playing the ball off the left instep, balancing too much weight on the right side and leaning away from the target, setting the hands a few inches behind the ball, tensing the arms at address, and trying to chip like you putt can cause a thin chip shot.

**Cures:** To prevent hitting a thin chip, play the ball near the midpoint in a very narrow, slightly open stance, set your hands a couple of inches ahead of the ball, place approximately 60 percent of your weight on the left foot, let your arms hang down naturally in a tension-free address position, hinge the right wrist in the backswing, and hold the hinged position on the downswing. These corrections will ensure that you hit the ball slightly on the descent and make clean, crisp clubface-to-ball contact at impact.

**Fighting a Common Putting Problem**—*The Pulled Putt* (A putt that rolls straight left of target).

**Causes:** Aligning your club and body too far left of target, placing too much weight on your left foot, keeping your left eye over a spot ahead of the ball, pulling the club back outside the target line, and using your hands to manipulate the putter through impact can all cause you to pull putts.

**Cures:** To cure your pull problem, set your body square to the target line and aim the putter-face directly at the hole. Play the ball opposite your left heel with your eyes directly over the ball or behind it and over the target line. Control the stroke with your arms and shoulders, and focus on putter-direction so the putter stays square to the hole from the start of the stroke to its finish.

.  .  .

Facing your swing and shot-making faults head-on is a good thing. Furthermore, accepting the challenge to fix them will make you a stronger individual and better golfer. But it's also important to escape from the course and relax

Tiger and I used our sessions away from the course—like this dinner at my home—to relax and talk about life issues more than golf issues.

from time to time. Sometimes short layoffs help the quality of one's game. Don't worry: Old Man Par will be waiting for you to challenge him, and there will always be beautiful golf days ahead.

In finishing this book, I want to wish you all the best of luck in your quest to improve your golf game. I have given you all of the most important information I have learned over the years, tips that I have invented myself to help students, and myself, shoot lower scores. The irony is, much of what I know I learned from those players—young and old—who came to me for lessons. One of those players was Tiger Woods. He trusted the instructions I gave him and I am proud that once he implemented particular technical movements into his swing, they worked, and worked well. His record is proof of that. But Tiger himself was innovative and his genius rubbed off on me. So even though I possess a signed photograph of Tiger, with an inscription from him thanking me in his own words for my work, it is now my turn to pay homage to this one-of-a-kind golfer. Thank you, Tiger, I owe you a great deal of gratitude, too.

This signed photograph of Tiger Woods is something I look at from time to time as a reminder that hard work pays off.

To John Andrews,
Thanks for all your
help over the years.
Tiger Woods

# BIOGRAPHICAL
# PROFILES

**A**uthor **John Anselmo** is a California-based golf instructor best known for teaching junior players—namely Tiger Woods.

Anselmo, who once played the professional circuit with Sam Snead and Ben Hogan, gave Tiger his first lesson at the Los Alamitos Golf Course in Cypress, California, when the youngster was ten years old. Anselmo continued to teach Tiger on a regular basis until Tiger turned eighteen. In total, he gave Tiger around 350 lessons. He also played golf with him about twenty-five times—even offering tips after Tiger enrolled at Stanford and returned home for breaks.

During his long career Anselmo has given approximately one hundred thousand lessons and produced a stable of champions that has over two hundred wins. Today, Anselmo still teaches at Meadowlark. His most promising students include thirteen-year-old Billy Olsen and sixteen-year-old Dennis Chang.

Anselmo resides in Huntington Beach, California, with his wife, Janet. *"A-Game" Golf* is his first book published in the United States.

Coauthor **John Andrisani** is a former instruction editor at *GOLF Magazine*. He has written two books that analyze the power swing, and short game, of Tiger Woods. He also collaborated on two books with Tiger's present teacher, Butch Harmon.

Andrisani, an eight-handicap player, resides in Sarasota, Florida.

**Yasuhiro Tanabe** is a freelance photographer whose work appears regularly in *GOLF DIGEST* (Japan) magazine. His photographic book credits include *The Idiot's Guide to the Short Game,* by Jim McLean.

**Allen Welkis** is a freelance artist whose work appears in golf books and popular golf magazines.